Joan Elliott's
Native American
CROSS STITCH

We are but a thread in the web of life
Whatever we do to the web we do to ourselves
All things are bound together
All things are connected
(Chief Seattle)

David and Charles

To all Native Americans and their ancestors before them:
the treasure of your culture and heritage has graced the
land for thousands of years. With reverence and admiration,
I thank you for allowing me a brief glimpse into its many wonders.

A DAVID & CHARLES BOOK
David & Charles is a subsidiary of F+W (UK) Ltd.,
an F+W Publications Inc. company

First published in the UK in 2005

Distributed in North America
by F+W Publications, Inc.
4700 East Galbraith Road
Cincinnati, OH 45236
1-800-289-0963

A catalogue record for this book is available from the British Library.
ISBN 0 7153 2071 8

Executive editor Cheryl Brown
Desk editor Ame Verso
Art editor Prudence Rogers
Project editor and chart preparation Lin Clements
Photography Johnny Bouchier and Karl Adamson

Printed in China by SNP Leefng
for David & Charles
Brunel House   Newton Abbot   Devon

Visit our website at www.davidandcharles.co.uk

David & Charles books are available from all good bookshops; alternatively you can
contact our Orderline on (0)1626 334555 or write to us at FREEPOST EX2110, David
& Charles Direct, Newton Abbot TQ12 4ZZ (No stamp required UK mainland).

Contents

Introduction

'Weavers would add red for power and long life, white for peace and happiness, blue for sadness leading to wisdom and black for the end of the life cycle giving way to renewal.'

For countless generations Native Americans inhabited the vast lands of the 'New World': their story is filled with both magnificence and tragedy. From the woodlands of the Northeast across the vast Plains to the desert Southwest, thriving native culture produced some of the most exquisite and admired art and design ever created. These resourceful people were farmers, hunters, artists, craftsmen, writers, shamans and leaders. Adapting to their individual environments, the diverse groups developed unique languages and cultures. Over the course of thousands of years the strong relationship of the people to their environment and the respect they had for the magical powers of nature led to invaluable knowledge and faith in the resources of the earth and sky. They became expert stewards of the land and in return it yielded abundant crops, wildlife, and healing medicines. They prayed to the heavens for strength and guidance and were duly rewarded by the Great Spirit.

Profound changes would take place in the lives of Native Americans with the arrival of the Europeans in the 16th century. The newcomers brought opportunities for trade and commerce. In exchange for furs and skins, the Indians received trade cloth, glass beads, tools, knives and muskets. Likewise, the Indians imparted their insightful knowledge of agriculture to the settlers, which was an important survival factor in this foreign land. Despite these apparently amicable exchanges, in other ways the seeds were sown for a tragic change in the lives of all Native Americans. The most devastating changes that took place were the onset of previously unknown diseases which would decimate entire native populations, the encroachment of European expansionism on Indian lands, and the near extinction of the buffalo, the essential resource that supplied the western tribes with life-sustaining food and clothing.

Loss of territory progressed into the 1800s, with countless breaches of treaties and many instances of forced removal of Native Americans from their ancient lands. Most notably in the 1830s, the Indian Removal Act, also known as the 'Trail of Tears', forced the southern tribes on to reservations – limited barren tracts of land in Oklahoma. In 1890 the Wounded Knee Massacre in the west resulted in the same fate for the Sioux. This was the ultimate tragedy for those whose love of the land was so personal and who regarded it as a sacred right to live on that land. It is a sad legacy to have left the

original inhabitants with so little. Today there is a new awareness of this sorrowful time in America's history. The descendants of the brave people who endured this devastating period in history still carry the wisdom and experience of their ancestral culture told through ancient stories and their incredibly creative spirits.

To experience the landscape of the American Southwest is to open your eyes to the sense of being one with nature. It is a land filled with magical skies and rainbow-coloured earth and it becomes easy to understand the inspiration that Native Americans draw from the world around them. It is with this in mind that the designs for this book have been created. The sustaining power of many Southwest tribes is the Spirit world: daily activities, dreams and visions are all nurtured within the ancient web of life, creativity flourishing under its protection. Because of this connection to the spiritual realm,

'The sustaining power of many Southwest tribes is the Spirit world: daily activities, dreams and visions are all nurtured within the ancient web of life.'

'Native culture produced some of the most exquisite and admired art and design ever created.'

all things creative are naturally intertwined with the sense and beauty of the Great Spirit.

The union of spirit and daily life was ever present: no mundane chore was separate from this ethereal essence. Even clothing was chosen with regard to the heavens. Elaborate beading and fringing sanctified dresses and shirts, while colours chosen for blankets and robes had special meaning. Weavers would add red for power and long life, white for peace and happiness, blue for sadness leading to wisdom and black for the end of the life cycle giving way to renewal. Infants were carried in decorated cradle boards for both earthly and heavenly protection. Flowers and herbs provided the dyes for the weaver's hand-spun wool and the healing medicines of the shaman. No material used was without significance and as each artist set about their work, through their hands travelled the connective web to the Great Wheel of Life. On wedding days,

the soon-to-be-married couple were presented with special wedding baskets to bring abundance and happiness into their life together. As the basket maker worked, traditional step patterns were woven in contrasting colours to show the path they would now travel together as man and wife.

The art of storytelling was and is an inherent part of American Indian life. Legends and proverbs were seen as educational tools passed on by the elders to teach lessons of ethical behaviour and love of the natural and spirit worlds. Daily prayers were commonplace as each day was recognized as a gift from the Great Creator. Wisdom was imparted from generation to generation. Toys were often miniature versions of adult objects. Small tipis (tepees) and bows and arrows allowed the children to learn the meaning and uses of everyday objects, and always there was the ever-present teaching of respect for the land.

The rugs, jewellery and pottery of the Southwest peoples are probably their most easily recognized creations. Working and living in the arid mountains, the Navajo are world renowned for their exquisite silver and turquoise jewellery. Intricate squash blossom necklaces, handsomely engraved silver wrist cuffs, and simple large conchas (medallions) are hallmarks of their work. On huge outdoor looms, under brilliant blue skies the women of the Navajo nation weave magic into their rugs and blankets. Ancient patterns and modern adaptations spring to life as the yarns intertwine. It was the people from neighbouring pueblos who first taught the Navajo how to weave. High on the mesas in more than 30 villages live the Pueblos peoples and for almost 1,000 years their creative hands have produced distinctively beautiful pottery decorated with ancient symbols and patterns in rich earthen clay. To see a piece of this finely crafted ware is to look in amazement at the precise hand-painted images, each one carefully applied with the Great Spirit watching over.

Family life is an important part of Native American tradition. It is here that grandfathers impart their wisdom to the young ones and that children learn from the artists and teachers that surround them. Not only jewellery making but also pottery, basket and rug weaving and needle arts will be taught. Skills in beading, quillwork, weaving and quilting find regeneration in young hands. Today there is a renaissance of Native American artists, each one speaking the soulful story of their ancestors through their own unique artistic expression.

I hope that the designs in this book will spark your interest in exploring and understanding the many enchanting aspects of Native American culture and art. I know that my small scope of knowledge about these courageous and spiritual people is ever anxious to be expanded. As you stitch the projects I wish for you abundant inspiration and awareness of the sacred energy that flows through each of us as we put our hands to our creative tasks.

'Working and living in the arid mountains, the Navajo are world renowned for their exquisite silver and turquoise jewellery.'

'To experience the landscape of the American Southwest is to open your eyes to the sense of being one with nature.'

Indian Maiden

The greatest strength is gentleness
(Iroquois)

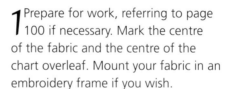

A beautiful Indian maiden whispers softly to the delicate creature in her palm. Dressed in a magnificent woven robe and a swirling skirt the rich colour of the setting sun, she shares a message of hope and renewal.

The spiritual significance of the hummingbird is intricately woven into the legends of many Native American tribes. For some, it represents optimism and tenderness, while others see this tiny dancer as a messenger linking nature and the Native peoples to the Spirit world.

Combined with silver, copper and jet, her costume and jewellery are adorned with delicate turquoise beads. Navajo legend has it that this rich blue stone is a bit of the sky that has fallen to Earth. In her other hand she holds a *pahos*, or prayer stick, which she will plant at the sacred site of a freshwater spring to send prayers to the Creator. The backdrop of a shimmering August moon is interwoven with the symbols of abundance (mountains), wisdom (medicine man's eye) and gentle strength (bear).

 Materials

- 58 x 48cm (23 x 19in) Fiddler's Light 14-count Aida
- DMC stranded cotton (floss) as listed in chart key
- Tapestry needle size 24 and a beading needle
- Kreinik #4 braid: 032 pearl (3 spools); 102 vatican (3 spools) and 191 pale yellow (1 spool)
- Mill Hill glass seed beads: 02014 black and 02038 brilliant copper
- Mill Hill Magnifica™ glass beads: 10028 silver and 10079 brilliant teal

Stitch count 243h x 187w
Design size 44 x 34cm (17½ x 13½in)

1 Prepare for work, referring to page 100 if necessary. Mark the centre of the fabric and the centre of the chart overleaf. Mount your fabric in an embroidery frame if you wish.

2 Start stitching from the centre of the chart and fabric, using two strands of stranded cotton (floss) for full and three-quarter cross stitches. Work the French knot for the bird's eye using one strand of black wound twice around the needle. Following the chart colours, use two strands for long stitches in the hair ornament feathers and prayer stick. Use one strand to stitch all Kreinik #4 braid cross stitches, long stitches, and backstitches. Work all other long stitches and backstitches with one strand. Using a beading needle and matching thread, attach the beads (see page 102) according to the chart.

3 Once all the stitching is complete, finish your picture by mounting and framing (see page 103).

Indian Maiden
DMC stranded cotton
Cross stitch

											Kreinik #4 Braid
■ 300	Z 318	356	← 415	╱ 436	T 598	729	734	◎ 3753	3777	3830	□ 032 pearl
⊡ 310	320	367	N 434	437	676	732	— 738	3755	3799	3835	102 vatican
∧ 317	╲ 322	◉ 400	435	+ 677	I 733	597	3747	V 3776	╱ 3829	• blanc	● 191 pale yellow

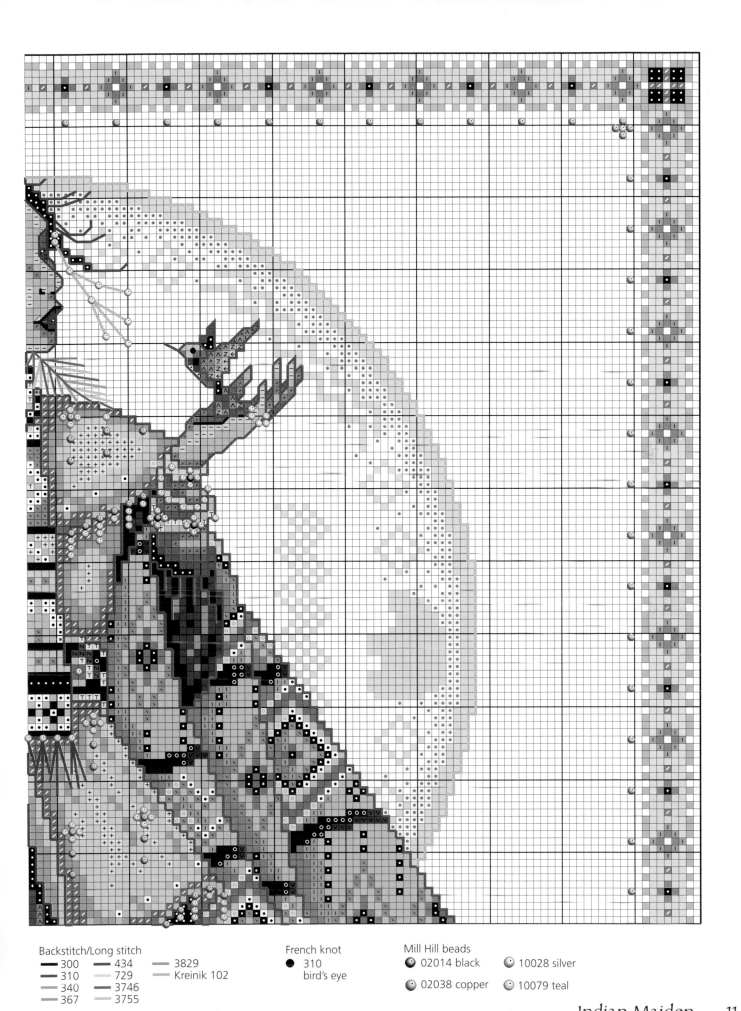

Backstitch/Long stitch
— 300   — 434   — 3829
— 310   — 729   — Kreinik 102
— 340   — 3746
— 367   — 3755

French knot
● 310
bird's eye

Mill Hill beads
◉ 02014 black   ◉ 10028 silver
◉ 02038 copper   ◉ 10079 teal

Indian Maiden
DMC stranded cotton
Cross stitch

											Kreinik #4 Braid
■ 300	Z 318	356	← 415	╱ 436	T 598	729	734	◉ 3753	3777	3830	032 pearl
⊡ 310	320	367	N 434	437	676	732	− 738	3755	3799	3835	102 vatican
∧ 317	╲ 322	◉ 400	435	597	+ 677	I 733	3747	V 3776	╱ 3829	• blanc	⦿ 191 pale yellow

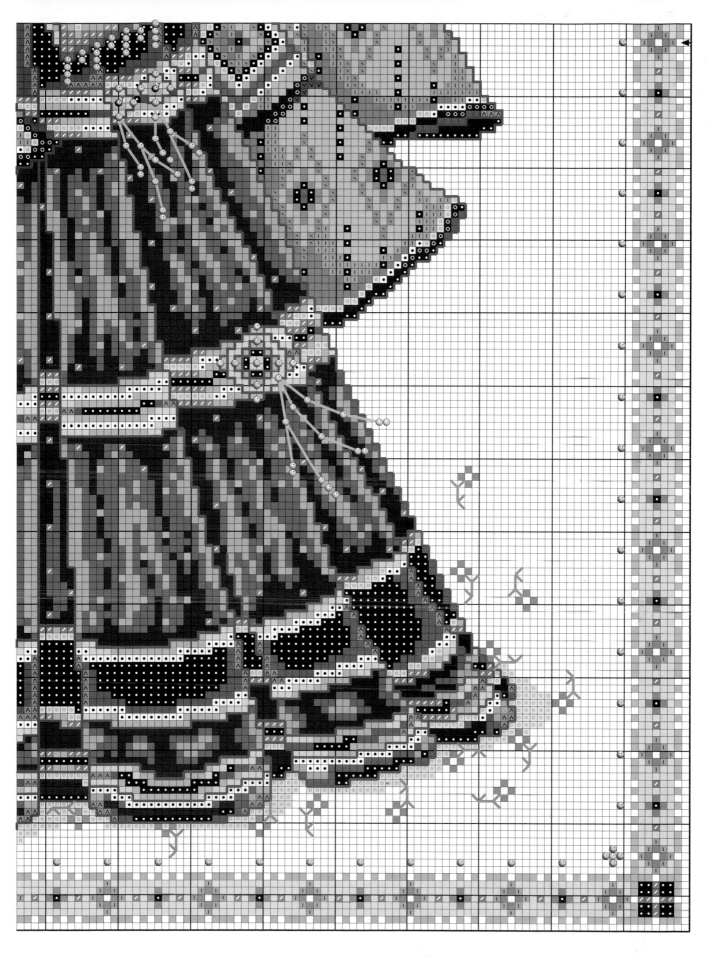

Backstitch/Longstitch
— 300   — 434   — 3829
— 310   — 729   — Kreinik 102
— 340   — 3746
— 367   — 3755

French knot
● 310
bird's eye

⊙ 02014 black   ⊙ 10028 silver

⊙ 02038 copper   ⊙ 10079 teal

Indian Maiden   13

Daily Inspirations

The heavens give us each a song
(Ute)

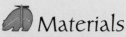

Materials

For each hanging

- 30.5 x 25.5cm (12 x 10in) antique white 14-count Aida
- DMC stranded cotton (floss) as listed in chart key
- Tapestry needle size 24
- Ultrasuede®: two pieces 23 x 30.5cm (9 x 12in) for backing and border and one strip 76cm x 6mm (30 x ¼in) for hanging
- Lightweight iron-on interfacing
- Fusible web
- Assorted feathers and beads
- Four decorative buttons
- 30cm (11½in) wooden dowel 6mm (¼in) diameter
- Permanent fabric glue

Stitch count (each hanging)
99h x 71w
Design size 18 x 12.9cm (7 x 5in)

Many words of wisdom have been passed down through generations of Native Americans honouring the spirit and sacred beauty in all people. The three hangings in this chapter carry messages of inspiration from three different tribes.

The Ute of the Southwest beautifully remind us, 'the heavens give us each a song'. What better way to encourage self-expression and pride in ourselves as individuals? From the Cherokee Nation of the Southeast, we are advised to 'judge not by the heart, but by the eye'. From the Northeast, the Tuscarora tribe brings us inspiration that reveals the true beauty of the

spoken word. 'Words are the voice of the heart', is a message of caring, faith, and commitment.

The hangings are easily stitched using just cross stitch, backstitch and French knots. The flower motifs chosen are reminiscent of the colourful beading, quill work and appliqué that many tribes used on their clothing and other objects. Decorative beads and feathers, symbols of prayer and ideas, create the perfect finishing touch.

1 Prepare for work, referring to Techniques page 100 if necessary. Mark the centre of the fabric and circle the centre of the chart with a pen. Mount your fabric in an embroidery frame if you wish.

2 Start stitching from the centre of the chart and fabric, using two strands of stranded cotton (floss) for full and three-quarter cross stitches. Following the chart colour changes, work French knots using two strands wrapped once around the needle. Work backstitch lettering using two strands and all other backstitches with one.

➤ Violet is the colour of healing and wisdom and seemed a fitting choice for these poetic words. The corner squares of this design contain butterflies, the symbol of everlasting life, and the sun, a symbol for warmth, growth and happiness.

Making Up a Hanging

1 Once all stitching is complete, make up into a hanging by first using pinking shears to carefully trim the 23 x 30.5cm (9 x 12in) background fabric close to all four edges. To create a casing for the dowel, with the fabric positioned vertically, turn the top edge to the back by 2.5cm (1in) and glue carefully close to the pinked edge. To create the bottom fringe, draw a line on the back of the fabric 2.5cm (1in) from the bottom edge. With very sharp scissors, carefully cut the fringe to this line, using the pinked indentations as your guide.

2 Trim the finished embroidery to within seven rows of the border edge. Cut a piece of interfacing to the same size and fuse to the wrong side of the embroidery following the manufacturer's instructions. Cut a piece of fusible web to the same size and place it on the wrong side of the embroidery – ensure the edges do not overlap the trimmed embroidery. Centre your work between the top folded edge and the top of the fringed edge. Press to fuse the embroidery and background fabric together.

3 Cut four lengths of contrasting border fabric each 30.5 x 1cm (12in x ⅜in) and place around the embroidery leaving four rows of Aida showing. Trim as necessary and carefully glue down. Glue a decorative button at each corner.

4 Insert the dowel through the top casing. To make the hanging cord, attach the strip of Ultrasuede® by tying in a knot around each dowel end, being sure to leave at least 18cm (7in) of suede hanging down on each side. Thread beads and feathers on the ends of the suede as desired.

◄ The rich red of the flowers represents the sun, faith and knowledge. In the corners are patterns that signify the cycle of life and a good future. By learning to see correctly, we rise to a brighter tomorrow.

The Heavens Give Us Each a Song
DMC stranded cotton

Cross stitch

■ 301	■ 792	☐ 794	■ 3362	☐ 3364	
■ 310	✕ 793	☐ 992	⊙ 3363	• blanc	

Backstitch
— 792
— 3362

French knots
● 792
○ blanc

Judge Not by the Heart But by the Eye
DMC stranded cotton
Cross stitch

▣ 310	⊙ 367	597	3857	3859	
319	368	3829	⊥ 3858	• blanc	

Backstitch
— 319
— 3857

French knots
● 3857

Words are the Voice of the Heart
DMC stranded cotton
Cross stitch

■ 310	■ 501	■ 503	■ 783	■ 3839
■ 434	+ 502	V 782	■ 920	· blanc

Backstitch
— 434

French knots
● 434

➤ The golden cactus flower in this hanging represents love and courtship, while the arrows in the corner motifs are symbolic of the heart line and life force.

Apache Wedding

*Do not walk behind me, I may not lead
Do not walk in front of me, I may not follow
Walk beside me that we may be as one*
(Ute)

In a ceremony held in the quiet evening hours, Native American families and guests would provide wedding baskets filled with abundant food to nourish the bride and groom and marriage blankets to keep them warm and protected.

Surrounded by a border worked in the colours of twilight, the Apache Wedding blessing that graces this heirloom sampler speaks of the safe-keeping and companionship that exists within the sacred bond of marriage. A softly toned sky-band border symbolizes the path to happiness. Dusty mauve wildflowers of the arid mountains suggest the blossoming of the couple's new life together. In rich detail, delicate beads dot the centres of small crosses representing crossing paths and the people met along the way. The two are now one and they journey forward together.

The ensemble is completed with a picture frame for remembering this special occasion, a pretty card to send personal wishes of love, and a little place card to welcome and seat your guests.

➤ Create a personalized tribute for a special couple on their wedding day with this heartfelt blessing. In each piece of the ensemble, tiny pearls, iridescent beads and traditional border patterns echo the beading and embroidery traditions of the first Americans.

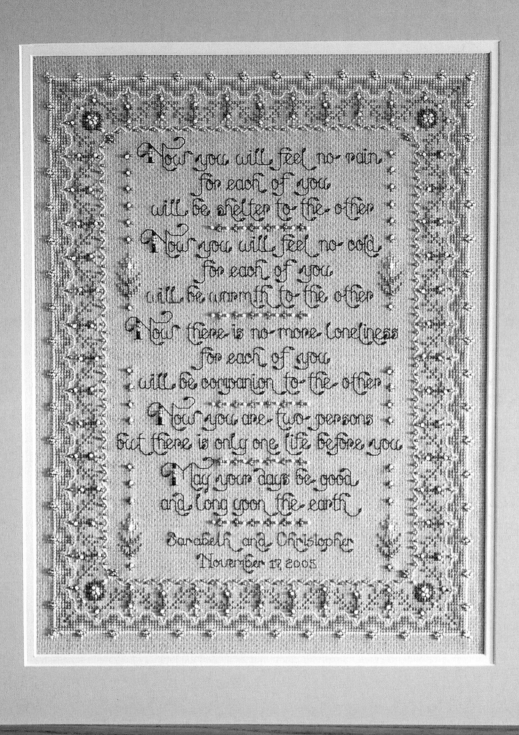

Now you will feel no rain
for each of you
will be shelter to the other

Now you will feel no cold
for each of you
will be warmth to the other

Now there is no more loneliness
for each of you
will be companion to the other

Now you are two persons
but there is only one life before you

May your days be good
and long upon the earth

Sarabeth and Christopher
November 19 2005

For each of you
will be shelter
to the other

Materials

- 50 x 43cm (20 x 17in) flax 14-count Aida (DMC code 738)
- Tapestry needle size 24 and a beading needle
- DMC stranded cotton (floss) as listed in chart key
- Mill Hill glass seed beads: 00479 white and 00561 ice green
- Mill Hill antique glass beads: 03007 silver moon

Stitch count 205h x 157w
Design size 37.2 x 28.5cm
(14½ x 11¼in)

Wedding Sampler

1 Prepare for work, referring to page 100 if necessary. Mark the centre of the fabric and chart. Mount your fabric in an embroidery frame if you wish.

2 Start stitching from the centre of the chart on pages 28–29, using two strands of stranded cotton (floss) for full cross stitches. Use two strands for white backstitches and one strand for backstitched lettering and three-quarter cross stitches and one strand wrapped once around the needle for French knots. Using a beading needle and matching thread, attach the beads (see page 102) following the chart. Use the alphabet charted here to stitch the names and wedding date. Plan the letters on graph paper first to ensure they fit the space.

3 Once all stitching is complete, finish your wedding sampler by mounting and framing (see page 103).

Wedding Sampler Alphabet
DMC stranded cotton
Three-quarter cross stitch

■ 336 (or colour of your choice)

Backstitch
— 336

French knots
● 336

Wedding Card

This pretty little card is very quick to stitch. Working on an 18 x 20cm (7 x 8in) piece of 18-count oatmeal Rustico Aida (Zweigart code 3292/054/51), follow the chart below, using two strands of stranded cotton (floss) for cross stitches and white backstitches and one strand for backstitch lettering. Using a beading needle and matching thread, attach the beads (see page 102). Mount your embroidery in a suitable double-fold card (see page 102).

Stitch count 41h x 57w **Design size** 5.8 x 8cm (2¼ x 3⅛in)

Place Card

Matching place cards are quick to stitch and will complete your wedding ensemble. Stitch the small rosette from the bottom border of the wedding card (charted below) on antique brown 14-count perforated paper (Mill Hill code PP3). Cut out the design leaving two rows all round. Purchase blank place cards – you can have them engraved, do the lettering by hand, or print them out on the computer in the style of your choice. Attach the embroidery to the card with double-sided adhesive tape and add a small bow to finish.

Stitch count 15h x 7w
Design size 1.3 x 2.7cm (½ x 1in)

Wedding Card
DMC stranded cotton

Cross stitch		Backstitch	
▢	157	▬	3371
▩	315	▬	B5200
▩	501		
▢	502	**French knots**	
v	793	●	3371
×	794		
▩	3371		
+	3726	**Mill Hill beads**	
▢	3727	☉	00479 white
•	B5200	☉	00561 ice green

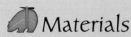

Materials

- 38 x 33cm (15 x 13in) flax 14-count Aida (DMC code 738)
- Tapestry needle size 24 and a beading needle
- DMC stranded cotton (floss) as listed in chart key
- Mill Hill glass seed beads: 00479 white and 00561 ice green
- Mill Hill antique glass beads: 03007 silver moon
- 26.5 x 22cm (10½ x 8½in) lightweight iron-on interfacing
- Two pieces 26.5 x 22cm (10½ x 8½in) mounting board
- Sharp craft knife
- 26.5 x 22cm (10½ x 8½in) cotton wadding (batting)
- 152cm (60in) decorative beaded edging
- Permanent fabric glue
- Double-sided adhesive tape

Stitch count 133h x 109w
Design size 24 x 19.8cm
(9½ x 7¾in)

Picture Frame

1 Prepare for work, referring to page 100 if necessary. Mark the centre of the fabric and chart. Mount your fabric in an embroidery frame if you wish.

2 Start stitching from the centre of the chart opposite, using two strands of stranded cotton (floss) for cross stitches and backstitches. Using a beading needle and matching thread, attach the beads (see page 102) as on the chart. Once all stitching is complete, make up into a picture frame, as follows.

Making Up a Frame

1 Mark out a central rectangular window on one piece of mounting board by measuring in 6.3cm (2½in) from all four sides. Carefully cut out the window with a sharp craft knife, keeping corners sharp. Glue the wadding (batting) to the board, matching outside edges, and cut out the window in the wadding.

2 On the wrong side of the empty centre area of the embroidery, use a soft pencil and the fabric weave as a guide to draw a rectangle along the fourth row in from the embroidery's edge. Centre iron-on interfacing over the wrong side of the embroidery and fuse according to the manufacturer's instructions. Using sharp scissors cut a slit in the centre of the empty rectangle. Very carefully, and making sure not to cut beyond your pencil line, cut diagonally from the centre to each corner of the rectangle.

3 Centre the mounting board over the fabric with the prepared side facing the wrong side of the embroidery. Fold the triangles of fabric to the back of the board and secure with fabric glue. Fold the outer edges of the fabric to the back of the board and glue, mitring the corners so they lie flat.

4 Carefully glue the decorative beading around the outside of the frame and the inner edge of the window. Insert your photograph to show evenly through the window and tape it on to the back of the frame. Cover the back of the frame with the second piece of mounting board to finish.

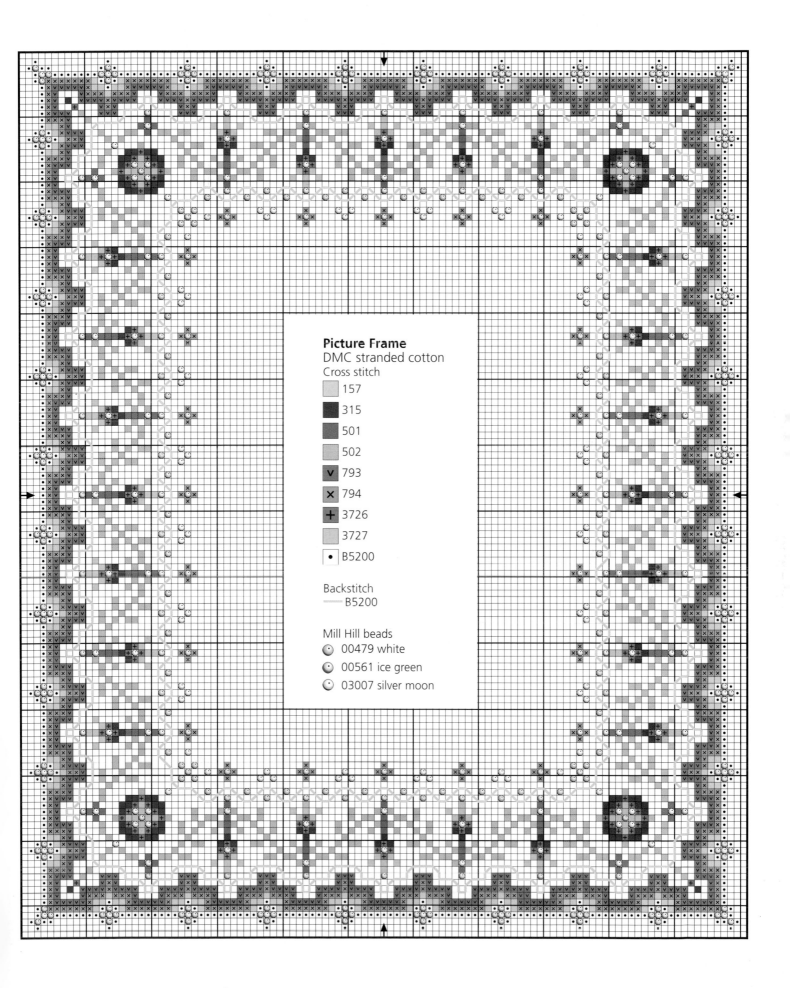

Picture Frame
DMC stranded cotton
Cross stitch

- 157
- 315
- 501
- 502
- v 793
- × 794
- + 3726
- 3727
- • B5200

Backstitch
— B5200

Mill Hill beads
- 00479 white
- 00561 ice green
- 03007 silver moon

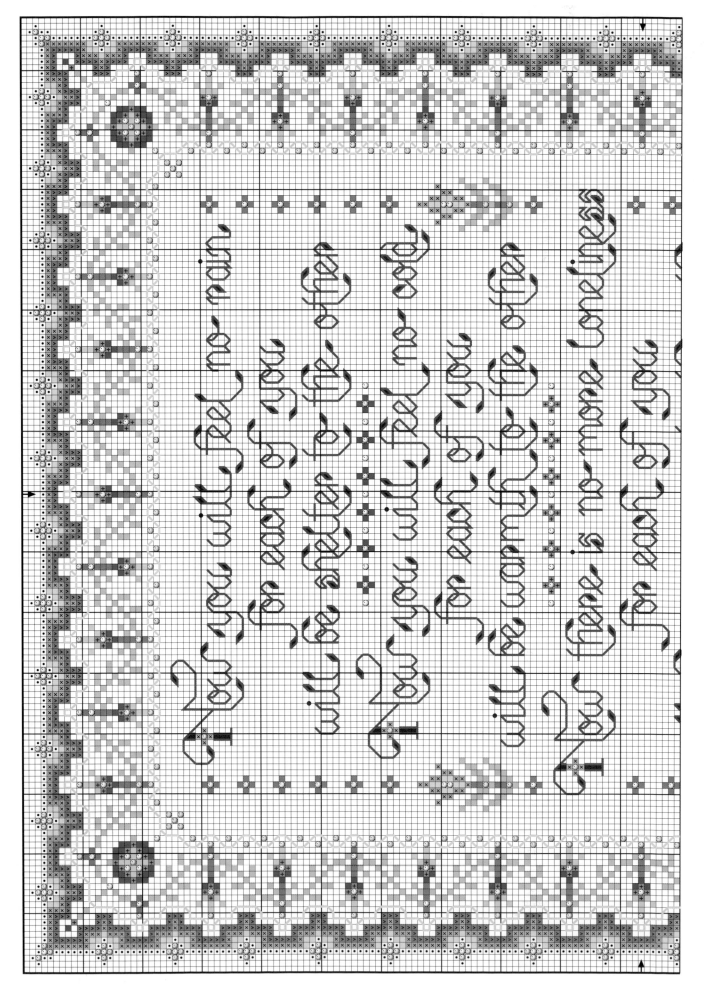

28　Apache Wedding

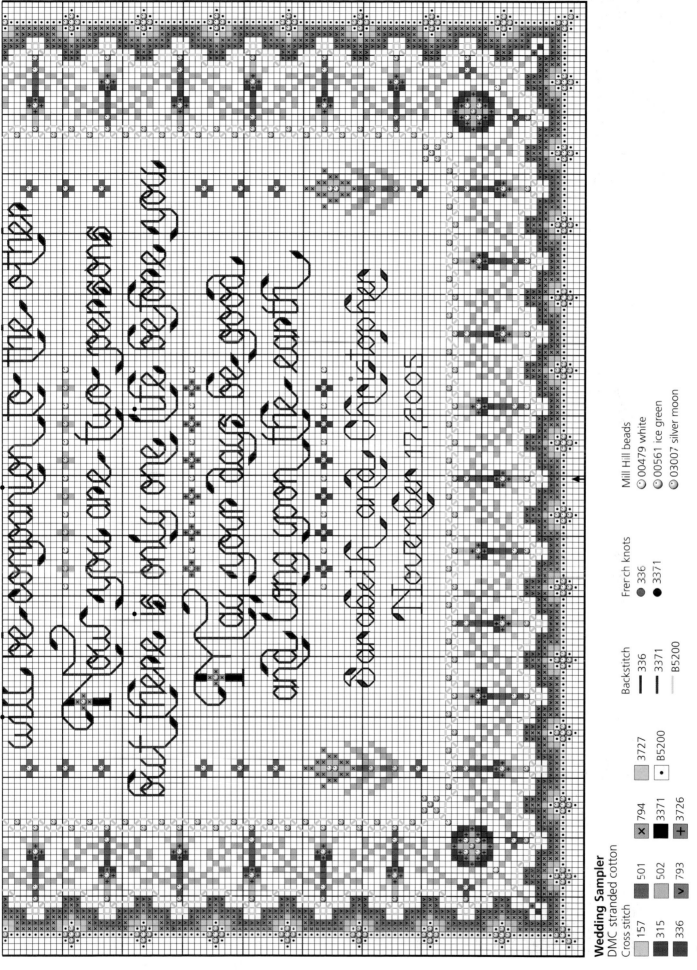

Wedding Sampler
DMC stranded cotton

Cross stitch

157	501	3727	
315	502	■ B5200	
336	793 v	3726	
	794 X	3371 ■	
	3371	B5200 ·	

Backstitch
— 336
— 3371
--- B5200

French knots
● 336
● 3371

Mill Hill beads
⊙ 00479 white
◎ 00561 ice green
◉ 03007 silver moon

Beaded Treasures

I have been to the end of the earth
I have been to the end of the waters
I have been to the end of the sky
I have been to the end of the mountains
I have found none that are not my friend
(Navajo)

The Navajo people began making exquisite silver and turquoise jewellery in the mid-1800s. The ornaments they created contained elements of the earth and the sky – two important factors in the concept of the continual circle of life and spiritual communication.

Using the colour of a clear azure sky and the soft greens of the grasses below, the central motif in this jewellery collection is symbolic of the spirit of the four directions and the continuing cycle of life. This eternal symbol guides the traveller through life's path, which is seen in the surrounding borders. Glass seed beads the colour of turquoise stone and delicate silver dewdrops combine with sparkling silver threads bringing the precious ancient materials to mind. The matching fringed bag based on the traditional medicine bag will keep your jewellery organized during your travels, while a beaded photo case provides the perfect way to preserve your memories when you return.

➤ This lovely pendant and cuff would make wonderful accessories, whether worn with a simple black dress or a pair of jeans and can be kept in the fringed jewellery bag when not in use. The photo case also features sparkling beads and metallic threads and all the designs are easy to stitch as a treat for yourself or to give as gifts.

Materials

For Pendant and Bracelet

- Half a sheet of 14-count clear plastic canvas

- Tapestry needle size 24 and a beading needle

- DMC stranded cotton (floss) as listed in chart key

- Kreinik #4 Very Fine Braid 001HL silver hi lustre

- Mill Hill glass seed beads: 00081 jet; 02008 sea breeze and 02010 ice

- Mill Hill pebble glass beads for necklace: 05021 silver and 05270 bottle green

- 76cm (30in) black satin cord

- One small decorative button

- Black felt or Ultrasuede® for backing

- Permanent fabric glue

Stitch count Pendant 29h x 29w; Bracelet 85h x 19w
Design size Pendant 5.2 x 5.2cm (2 x 2in); Bracelet 15.4 x 3.4cm (6 x 1½in)

Pendant and Bracelet

1 Prepare for work, referring to page 100 if necessary. Both the pendant and bracelet will fit on the same half sheet of plastic canvas. Mark the centre of each chart (page 35).

2 Start stitching from the centre of each chart, using one strand for Kreinik 001HL cross stitches and two strands of stranded cotton (floss) for other cross stitches. Use one strand for backstitches. Using a beading needle and matching thread, attach the beads (see page 102) as on the chart. Once all stitching is complete, cut out each piece leaving one row of canvas around the designs. Using four strands of black thread, overcast stitch the last row of canvas around each design to create a neat edge.

3 To make up the pendant, sew on a large bead at the top for stringing the black satin cord. Add Mill Hill pebble glass beads to the cord as desired and tie the ends in a knot.

To make up the bracelet, sew a small button to one end. Cut 7.6cm (3in) of black satin cord and form into a loop by stitching the ends together. Sew the loop to the opposite end of the bracelet (ends pointing to centre of wrong side), adjusting the size to fit your wrist.

4 To finish, on the back of each piece, draw a thin bead of glue along the silver-stitched edge, avoiding the overcast edge. Place each piece on the backing fabric or felt. When the glue has dried completely, trim the fabric close to the edge with sharp scissors.

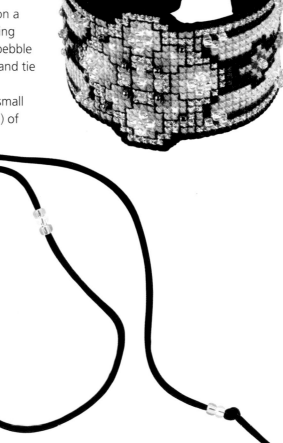

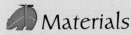

Materials

- 25.4 x 20.3cm (10 x 8in) white 14-count Aida
- Tapestry needle size 24 and a beading needle
- DMC stranded cotton (floss) as listed in chart key
- Kreinik #4 Very Fine Braid 001HL silver hi lustre
- Mill Hill glass seed beads: 00081 jet; 02008 sea breeze and 02010 ice
- Two pieces 23 x 12.7cm (9 x 5in) Ultrasuede® to tone with embroidery
- Lightweight iron-on interfacing
- Fusible web (see Suppliers)
- 51cm (20in) length of decorative cord to tone with embroidery
- Two small decorative buttons
- Permanent fabric glue

Stitch count 69h x 45w
Design size 12.7 x 7.6cm (5 x 3in)

Jewellery Bag

1 Prepare for work, referring to page 100 if necessary. Mark the centre of the fabric and chart (page 35). Mount fabric in a frame if you wish.

2 Start stitching from the centre of the chart, using one strand for Kreinik 001HL cross stitches and two strands of stranded cotton (floss) for other cross stitches. Use one strand for backstitches. Using a beading needle and matching thread, attach the beads (see page 102).

3 Once all stitching is complete cut iron-on interfacing the size of the embroidery and fuse it to the wrong side following the manufacturer's instructions. Trim the finished embroidery to within six rows of the border edge and fold these rows over to the back.

4 Holding one piece of Ultrasuede® vertically, on the wrong side draw a line 3.8cm (1½in) from the bottom edge. Fold over the top edge to the wrong side by 1.25cm (½in) and press. Align the bottom edge of the second piece with the drawn line on the first, wrong sides facing. Tack (baste) to hold in place. Using the edge of the second piece of Ultrasuede® as a guide, stitch a 1.25cm (½in) seam across the bottom and up two sides, leaving the top edge free – this leaves 3.8cm (1½in) of fabric free at the top for the flap and at the bottom for the fringe. Use pinking shears to pink all four edges. Using the pinking notches as a guide, cut the fabric to create a fringe, stopping just before the bottom stitching line. On the front of the bag, sew on a button at the centre 2cm (¾in) from the top folded edge. Turn the top flap to the front and, locating the sewn button beneath, cut a slit in the fabric to pass the button through for closing.

5 With the bag closed, centre the embroidery on the front. Cut a piece of fusible web the size of the prepared embroidery and sandwich it between the wrong side of the embroidery and the right side of the bag. Press to fuse. Using a thin line of fabric glue attach the decorative cord around the edge of the embroidery, starting and ending at centre bottom and sewing on a small button where the ends meet.

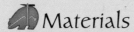

Materials

- 20.3 x 25.4cm (8 x 10in) white 14-count Aida
- Tapestry needle size 24 and a beading needle
- DMC stranded cotton (floss) as listed in chart key
- Kreinik #4 Very Fine Braid 001HL silver hi lustre
- Mill Hill glass seed beads: 00081 jet; 02008 sea breeze and 02010 ice
- 20.3 x 45.7cm (8 x 18in) Ultrasuede® to tone with embroidery for backing
- Lightweight iron-on interfacing
- Fusible web (see Suppliers)
- 51cm (20in) length of black suede braiding
- ½m (½yd) of 3mm (⅛in) wide black satin ribbon
- One small decorative button
- Permanent fabric glue
- 10 x 15.2cm (4 x 6in) ready-made photo pages (from stationery and craft stores)

Stitch count 43h x 69w
Design size 7.8 x 12.5cm (3 x 5in)

Photo Case

1 Prepare for work, referring to page 100 if necessary. Mark the centre of the fabric and chart opposite. Mount fabric in a frame if you wish.

2 Start stitching from the centre of the chart, using one strand for Kreinik 001HL cross stitches and two strands of stranded cotton (floss) for other cross stitches. Use one strand for backstitches. Using a beading needle and matching thread, attach the beads (see page 102).

3 Once all stitching is complete make up into a photo case. Cut a piece of iron-on interfacing 2.5cm (1in) larger all round than the embroidery and fuse to the wrong side according to the manufacturer's instructions. Trim the embroidery to within seven rows of the stitched border.

4 Fold the piece of Ultrasuede® in half lengthways and press to form a crease. Lay the fabric flat and fold the two ends in towards the centre crease by 10cm (4in). Tack (baste) in place. Stitch the unfolded edges together with matching sewing thread. Use pinking shears to pink the sewn sides close to the edge.

5 Fold the stitched case in half, pockets on the inside. Cut a piece of fusible web the size of the trimmed embroidery. Centre the embroidery on the outside of the folded case, sandwiching the web between the case and the wrong side of the embroidery. Press to fuse. Using a thin line of fabric glue, attach the suede braiding around the edge of the trimmed Aida, beginning and ending at centre bottom. Cut the length of satin ribbon in half and glue it to the case with the braid, attaching a small button to hide raw ends. At the centre of the back edge, attach the other half of the ribbon by turning over 1.25cm (½in) and gluing in place. Slip the photo pages into the inside pockets of the case and tie the ribbon ends in a bow.

Pendant

Jewellery Bag

Beaded Treasures
DMC stranded cotton
Cross stitch   Backstitch
⬛ 310   — 310
➕ 320
◻ 341
◻ 368
◻ 597
⊙ 598
⬛ 3857
• blanc
◻ Kreinik 001HL

Mill Hill beads
◕ 00081 jet
◔ 02008 sea breeze
◑ 02010 ice

Photo Case

Bracelet

Baby Blessings

The ones that matter most are the children
They are the true human beings
(Lakota)

Golden morning stars glitter amongst a gathering of woodland babies enclosed in a sky-band the colours of the breaking dawn. Cuddly soft and new to the world, these tiny creatures will greet baby for a night of gentle slumber. In their innocence and wonder, children seem to have been delivered from above, a gift like no other.

A fluffy owlet bestows wisdom and truth; an inquisitive racoon is filled with curiosity. The tender fawn brings kindness and compassion and the clever fox is endowed with intelligence. Bringing messages of pure love and joy, two hummingbirds dart between the clouds.

The border squares of a darling cot blanket carry images of turtles, frogs and dragonflies – all symbols of springtime and creation. Join these winsome friends in celebration and stitch an adorable personalized sampler to commemorate baby's birth. Make up a soft block sized just right for baby's hands and use the same motifs to stitch the infant bibs. Create a delightful album cover to proudly show off the latest photos. Any of the pieces from this ensemble would make a sweet gift to commemorate the blessed event.

➤ These endearing little animals are suitable for making up a treasure trove of projects for any baby. You could also combine motifs from the charts for a nursery wall hanging or a nap-time door hanger. An alphabet helps you add your special baby's name.

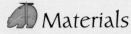 ## Materials

- Baby Alphabet Afghan antique white 18-count (see Suppliers)
- Tapestry needle size 24
- DMC stranded cotton (floss) as listed in chart key

Stitch counts Centre 190h x 158w; Border squares 27h x 27w
Design sizes Centre 53.6 x 44.5cm (21 x 17½in); Border squares (each) 7.6 x 7.6cm (3 x 3in)

Cot Blanket

1 Prepare for work, referring to page 100 if necessary. Mark the centre of the central Afghan panel and start stitching from the centre of the chart on pages 42–45, working full and three-quarter cross stitches over two threads using three strands. Note: some colours use more than one skein. For French knots use three strands wound once around the needle. Use two strands of DMC 801 for backstitch lettering and two strands of 470 for leaf stems. Use one strand for all other backstitches.

2 For the border, stitch the four border squares (charts on page 49) in the centres of the Afghan border squares, repeating the designs as necessary (see layout diagram below).

3 Once all stitching is complete, create a fringe around the blanket by running a machine stitch seven rows beyond the raised threads. Trim the blanket to within 3.2cm (1¼in) of the machine stitching and remove the threads up to the stitching line.

➤ Cot blanket layout of central panel and individual border squares.

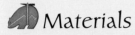

Materials

- 33 x 41cm (13 x 16in) antique white 14-count Aida
- Tapestry needle size 24 and a beading needle
- DMC stranded cotton (floss) as listed in chart key

Stitch count 116h x 156w
Design size 21 x 28cm
(8¼ x 11in)

Birth Sampler

1 Prepare for work, referring to page 100 if necessary. Mark the centre of the fabric and centre of the chart on pages 46–47. Mount your fabric in an embroidery frame if you wish.

2 Start stitching from the centre of the chart, using two strands of stranded cotton (floss) for full and three-quarter cross stitches. Following colour changes on the chart, use one strand for all backstitches and one strand wrapped twice around the needle for French knots. Use the alphabet on page 49 to stitch the baby's name and birth date. Plan the letters on graph paper first to ensure they fit the space.

3 Once all the stitching is complete, check for missed stitches and then finish your birth sampler by mounting and framing (see page 103 for advice).

Soft Block

For this delightful soft block you will need to stitch two of each of the three motifs charted on page 48 on six 20.3cm (8in) squares of antique white 14-count Aida. Use two strands of stranded cotton (floss) for cross stitches and one for backstitches and French knots.

To make up the block, trim each embroidery leaving 14 rows beyond the design edges. Cut iron-on interfacing the same size as each finished square and press on to the wrong side. Repeat for all squares.

Using one dragonfly square as a base, pin and tack (baste) two bunny squares opposite each other and two raccoon squares opposite each other on to each of the four edges of the base, right sides facing and all four animals facing the same direction. Stitch seams with a 1.25cm (½in) allowance, then press open. Fold each square upwards, sides meeting, right sides facing, and stitch matching sides together. To finish, pin and tack (baste) the remaining dragonfly square in place, stitching along three edges and leaving one open. Remove all pins, turn the block right side out, fill with stuffing and slipstitch the gap closed.

Stitch count (each design) 47 x 47
Design size 8.5 x 8.5cm (3⅜ x 3⅜in)

Memories Album

Using the charted design on page 48 (or one of the designs from the soft block), create this adorable photo album for precious memories of a new baby. Stitch it on antique white 14-count Aida. Extend the border ten rows at the bottom to create a space for adding the word 'Baby' or the baby's name using the alphabet on page 49. Plan the letters on graph paper first to ensure they fit the space. Attach the finished embroidery to the front of a purchased album using double-sided tape, or make up your own cloth-covered album following the instructions on page 103. Edge the embroidery by gluing on decorative braid, adding a pretty button where the ends meet.

Stitch count 57h x 47w
Design size 10.3 x 8.5cm (4 x 3⅜in)

Baby's Bibs

Any of the designs from the soft block would decorate a baby's bib beautifully, as these two charming examples show (see Suppliers for bib sources). You could also hand stitch the embroidery as a patch to the front of any bib or T-shirt. Stitch the design from the chart on page 48, following the stitching details from the Soft Block opposite. The animals could also be stitched and made up into pretty greetings cards stitched on 18-count Aida (see page 102 for mounting work in cards).

Stitch count (each design) 47 x 47
Design size 8.5 x 8.5cm (3⅜ x 3⅜in)

Cot Blanket - central panel

DMC stranded cotton

Cross stitch

▨ 156	E 334	╱ 434	↓ 471	⊥ 644	I 762	▨ 977	Y 3046	L 3811	< 3841	
T 167	+ 341	▨ 436	472	677	▨ 992	3078	— 3820	• blanc	
╱ 310	V 352	▨ 437	⊖ 640	N 738	▨ 938	╲ 993	3747	← 3822	
✳ 318	∧ 415	▨ 470	642	→ 754	▨ 976	✕ 3045	3755	⊙ 3826	

Backstitch
— 156
— 310
— 470
— 801
— 938

French knots
○ 470
○ 801
● 938
○ blanc

Cot Blanket - central panel
DMC stranded cotton
Cross stitch

156	E 334	╱ 434	↓ 471	⊥ 644	I 762	977	Y 3046	L 3811	< 3841		
T 167	+ 341	436	472	677	Z 801	992	3078	− 3820	• blanc		
╱ 310	V 352	437	⊖ 640	N 738	938	992	3747	← 3822			
✳ 318	⋀ 415	470	642	→ 754	976	X 3045	3755	O 3826			

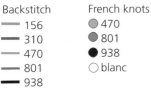

Backstitch
— 156
— 310
— 470
— 801
— 938

French knots
◑ 470
● 801
● 938
○ blanc

Bibs and Soft Block designs

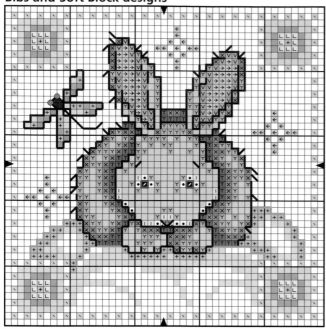 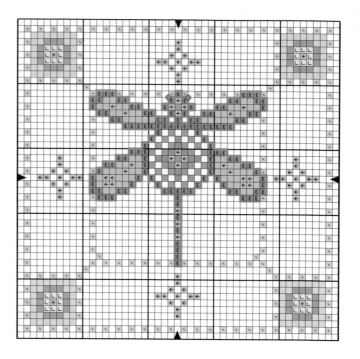

Memories Album

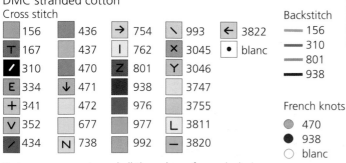

Bibs, Block and Album
DMC stranded cotton
Cross stitch

	156		436	→	754	\	993	←	3822
T	167		437	I	762	X	3045	•	blanc
/	310		470	Z	801	Y	3046		
E	334	↓	471		938		3747		
+	341		472		976		3755		
V	352		677		977	L	3811		
/	434	N	738		992	—	3820		

Backstitch
— 156
— 310
— 801
— 938

French knots
● 470
● 938
○ blanc

Note: you may not need all the colours for each design

Cot Blanket - border squares

Cot Blanket - border squares

DMC stranded cotton

Cross stitch

	156		436	→	754	\	993	←	3822	
T	167		437	I	762	X	3045	•	blanc	
/	310		470	Z	801	Y	3046			
E	334	↓	471		938		3747			
+	341		472		976		3755			
V	352		677		977	L	3811			
/	434	N	738		992	−	3820			

Backstitch

— 156
— 310
— 801
— 938

French knots
◯ 470
● 938
◯ blanc

Note: you may not need all the colours for each design

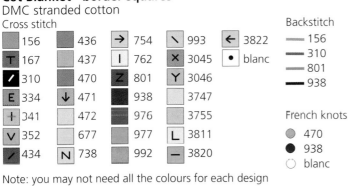

Birth Sampler Alphabet

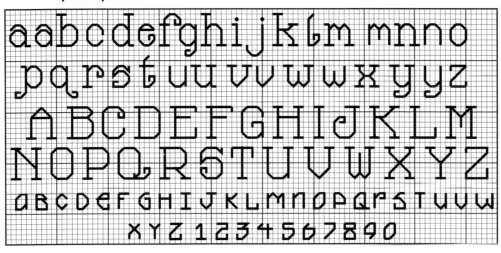

Native Borders

Truth makes friendship brighter
(Conestoga)

In wool and beads, grasses and porcupine quills the distinctive border designs of Native American textiles and baskets provide a wealth of inspiration for today's artists. Crossing paths and morning star designs handsomely accent a set of place mats, napkins and napkin rings which will bring the brilliant teal, rust and gold hues of the Southwest landscape to your table. These geometric patterns represent our journey through life and the guidance we receive along the way. Share their beauty with friends over a cup of tea or use the same

designs to make a pretty journal cover or bookmark for those quiet times alone.

For the bedroom and bathroom, the distinctive blossoms of the cactus worked in soft earthy tones of pink and green, and the unmistakable sunflower with its golden petals of friendship and warmth, accent a pair of pretty guest towels (shown on page 54). Why not make up a scented sachet and a useful trinket bowl for a sunny dresser display? You'll find a variety of uses for these timeless designs and each is easily repeated for larger projects.

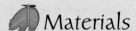

Materials

- Two 14-count Royal Classic country oatmeal place mats (see Suppliers)
- Two 14-count Royal Classic country oatmeal napkins (see Suppliers)
- Tapestry needle size 24
- DMC stranded cotton (floss) as listed in chart key

Stitch counts Place mat (each) 28h x 134w;
Napkin (each) 28h x 34w
Design sizes Place mat (each) 5 x 24.3cm (2 x 9½in);
Napkin (each) 5 x 6cm (2 x 2½in)

Geometric Place Mats and Napkins

To Work a Place Mat
Prepare for work, referring to page 100 if necessary. Mark the centre of the chart on page 53 and mount fabric in a frame if you wish. The design is placed on the left-hand side of the mat, so start working from the centre of the design 5cm (2in) above the fringed edge, using two strands of stranded cotton (floss) for cross stitches. Press from the back when all stitching is complete.

To Work a Napkin
Prepare for work and start from the centre of each the napkin design 5cm (2in) above the fringe at the bottom and left-hand side edge, using two strands of stranded cotton (floss) for cross stitches. Press from the back when complete.

➤ Sit down to a sunny breakfast or tea with these attractive place mats and napkins. A simple palette reflects the rich hues of the high desert and you will soon be able to make up as many as you need, bringing a fresh Southwest look to your table.

Napkin Rings

Complete your table setting with elegant napkin rings. Both designs will fit on a sheet of 14-count tan vinyl Aida. Leave ten rows of canvas between designs. From the centre of the border chart opposite, work 43 rows to either side. Once complete trim the right-hand side of the canvas, leaving one row beyond the embroidery and three rows on the left side. Trim long edges to within three rows usng pinking shears for a decorative edge. Create a ring by overlapping the straight edges with the single row edge on top. Tack (baste) together and cross stitch over the edge with two strands of DMC 3852 for the Morning Star design and DMC 975 for Crossing Paths.

Stitch count 28h x 86w   **Design size** 5 x 15.6cm (2 x 6in)

Morning Star Journal Cover

Make up a lovely journal cover by stitching the Morning Star design on a 30.5cm (12in) length of 8cm (3⅛in) white 16-count Aida band. Choose a journal to tone with the embroidery. Cut a piece of lightweight iron-on interfacing to cover the back of the embroidery and fuse in place according to the manufacturer's instructions. Centre the embroidery over the book cover and glue down with permanent fabric glue.

Stitch count 28h x 134w   **Design size** 4.5 x 21.3cm (1¾ x 8⅜in)

Crossing Paths Bookmark

Make a delightful bookmark using the Crossing Paths border. Stitch the design on a 28 x 15.2cm (11 x 6in) piece of Fiddler's Light 18-count Aida. Trim the finished embroidery eight rows beyond the design and create a fringe by machine stitching in toning thread, three rows beyond the embroidery all round. Pull out the threads up to the stitching line. Cut a piece of fusible web and white felt the same size as the finished design. Place the web on the back of the design, then the felt and iron to fuse.

Stitch count 28h x 134w   **Design size** 4 x 19cm (1½ x 7½in)

Crossing Paths Border (far left)
Morning Star Border (left)
DMC stranded cotton
Cross stitch

758		\	3778
831			3830
× 832		⊤	3848
964			3849
I 975			3852
— 3371		•	B5200

Crossing Paths Motif

Morning Star Motif

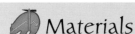

Materials

(for each border)

- White 14-count Royal Classic velour fingertip towel (see Suppliers)
- Tapestry needle size 24
- DMC stranded cotton (floss) as listed in chart key

Stitch counts (each border)
28h x 138w
Design sizes (each border)
5 x 25cm (2 x 10in)

Cactus and Sunflower Towels

Start by marking the centre of the chart (opposite) and the centre of the towel's Aida insert. Use two strands of stranded cotton (floss) for cross stitches and one for backstitches. Once stitching is complete, press from the back. Alternatively, work the design on Aida band and stitch the completed band to a towel of your choice.

Sunflower Trinket Bowl

Stitch a sunny bowl lid on a 15.2cm (6in) square of 14-count white Aida. Mark the centre of the fabric and centre of one of the border flowers in the chart opposite. Choose a trinket bowl to fit (see Suppliers) and mount the embroidery in the lid. Complete the Southwest look by gluing a strip of braided leather trim along the bowl rim, beginning and ending at the centre bottom. Attach a decorative button where the braid ends meet.

Stitch count 28h x 36w
Design size 5 x 6.5cm (2 x 2½in)

Sunflower Sachet

Make up a fragrant sachet by stitching the sunflower border on a 30cm (12in) length of 8cm (3⅛in) wide white 16-count Aida band. Once complete trim the ends to within 1.25cm (½in) of the embroidery.

Cut a piece of toning felt 25.4 x 10cm (10 x 4in) and pink the long sides. Cut fusible web the size of the trimmed embroidery, sandwich this between the wrong side of the band and felt and press to fuse. Cut two pieces of toning background felt 25.4 x 15.2cm (10 x 6in) and place the embroidery between these pieces. Stitch a 1.25cm (½in) seam all around leaving a gap for turning. Turn to the right side and stuff with polyester filling. Slipstitch the gap closed, leaving a small gap for tucking in the braid. Finish the edge by gluing or slipstitching 1m (1yd) of toning braid all round. Tuck in the ends and slipstitch closed. Attach two decorative buttons at centre top and bottom of the felt band.

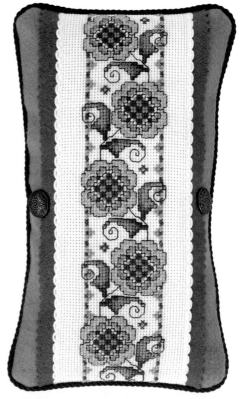

Stitch count 28h x 138w
Design size 4.5 x 22cm (1¾ x 8½in)

▨	732
+	733
▨	758
I	975
⊙	3362
O	3363
	3364
＼	3778
	3821
	3822
▨	3830
	3849
>	3852
•	blanc

Backstitch
— 934

Native American Alphabet

If we wonder often, the gift of knowledge will come
(Arapaho)

Armadillos, buffalo and cactus, an eagle in flight, a swift jackrabbit, a tipi (tepee) painted with the sign of the thunderbird, the master of the skies. American Indian life abounds with objects and symbols, from the sacred to the mundane. In earthen colours and glints of silver and jet, each letter of the alphabet is overflowing with the animals, crafts and symbols of tribal life, inviting us to take a closer look to see what else there may be to discover.

Can you find Kokopelli, the keeper of seeds? Do you see the playful otter, the harbinger of joy and laughter, or the mysterious Zuni raven that speaks for the shaman? Choose individual letters to create some special gifts such as a fringed wall hanging, a sweetly scented sachet or a precious trinket bowl (see overleaf). Try combining letters to make up a name plate for a special child and then have fun exploring all the elements of each letter together.

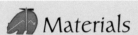 Materials

- 54 x 46cm (21 x 18in) natural 16-count Aida
- Tapestry needle size 24 and a beading needle
- DMC stranded cotton (floss) as listed in chart key
- Kreinik #4 Very Fine Braid 102 vatican
- Mill Hill Magnifica™ glass beads: 10004 jet and 10028 silver

Stitch count 261h x 202w
Design size 41.5 x 32cm (16¼ x 12½in)

Alphabet Sampler

1 Prepare for work, referring to page 100 if necessary. Mark the centre of the fabric and centre of the chart (pages 60–65). Mount the fabric in an embroidery frame if you wish.

2 Start stitching from the centre of the chart. Use one strand for Kreinik metallic thread cross stitches and backstitches. Use two strands of stranded cotton (floss) for all other full and three-quarter cross stitches and one strand for all other backstitches, except the white backstitches in letters N and H which use two strands. Use two strands for the long stitches in the feathers and one strand for all other black long stitches.

Use one strand for the black French knots, wound twice around the needle. Using a beading needle and matching thread, attach the beads (see page 102) following the chart colour changes.

3 Once all stitching is complete, finish your sampler by mounting and framing (see page 103).

Alphabet Sachet

Create a scented sachet featuring a letter from the main chart on a 15.2cm (6in) square of tea-dyed 28-count Monaco evenweave. Mark the centre of the fabric and charted letter. Follow the stitching instructions on page 56 but work over two fabric threads.

Once stitching is complete, make up into a sachet by cutting iron-on interfacing 2cm (¾in) larger than the design and pressing on the wrong side of the embroidery. Trim to within 1.25cm (½in) of the design edge. Cut two 15.2cm (6in) squares of backing fabric and a 25.4cm (10in) length of leather braiding. With top raw edges matching and on the right side of one of the fabric pieces, create a hanging loop by placing each end of the cord 3.8cm (1½in) from the sides of the fabric square. Tack (baste) in place. With right sides facing, stitch a 1.25cm (½in) seam all round leaving an opening at the bottom.

Turn to the right side and centre the embroidery on top, with a piece of fusible web the same size sandwiched between and fused to the sachet. Trim the embroidery edge with leather braid, starting and ending at centre bottom, attaching a button where the ends meet. Stuff with polyester filling or pot-pourri and slipstitch the opening.

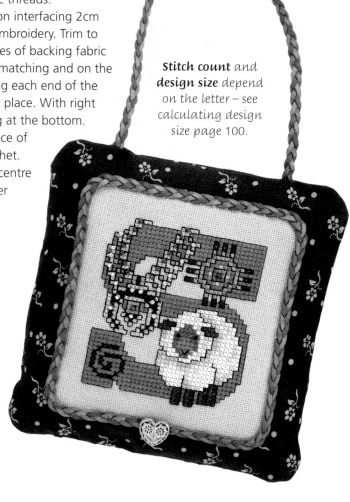

Stitch count and **design size** depend on the letter – see calculating design size page 100.

Alphabet Trinket Bowl

Stitch a handsome personalized trinket bowl lid on a 15.2cm (6in) square of 18-count Fiddler's Light Aida. Mark the centre of the fabric and charted letter and follow the stitching instructions on page 56. Mount the finished embroidery in a suitable bowl lid. Finish by gluing a strip of toning braided suede trim along the rim, beginning and ending at centre bottom. Attach a decorative button where the ends meet.

Stitch count and **design size** depend on the letter – see calculating design size page 100.

Alphabet Wall Hanging

Present a special friend with a monogrammed wall hanging (shown right) worked on 28-count oatmeal evenweave. Follow the stitching instructions on page 56, working over two fabric threads. Make up the hanging following the instructions on page 17 but use a 20.3 x 14cm (8 x 5½in) piece of toning Ultrasuede® and make the bottom fringe 3.2cm (1¼in) long.

Stitch count and **design size** depend on the letter – see calculating design size page 100.

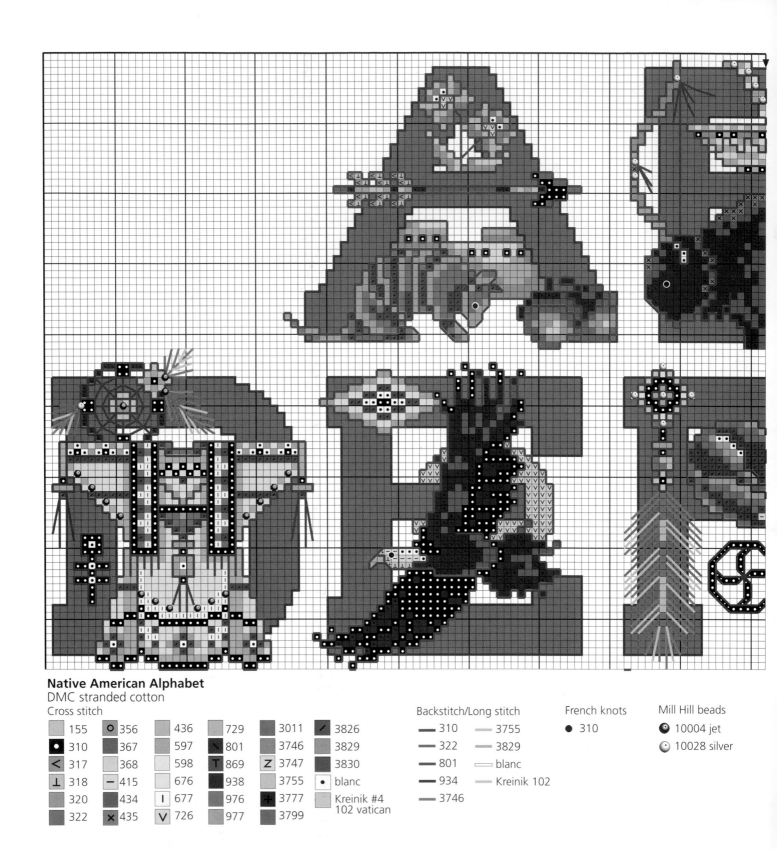

Native American Alphabet
DMC stranded cotton
Cross stitch

155	**O** 356	436	729	3011	**⁄** 3826
⬤ 310	367	597	**** 801	3746	3829
< 317	368	598	**T** 869	**Z** 3747	3830
⊥ 318	**−** 415	676	938	3755	**•** blanc
320	434	**I** 677	976	3777	**+** 3777
322	**×** 435	**V** 726	977	3799	Kreinik #4 102 vatican

Backstitch/Long stitch

— 310	— 3755
— 322	— 3829
— 801	— blanc
— 934	— Kreinik 102
— 3746	

French knots

● 310

Mill Hill beads

◉ 10004 jet
◉ 10028 silver

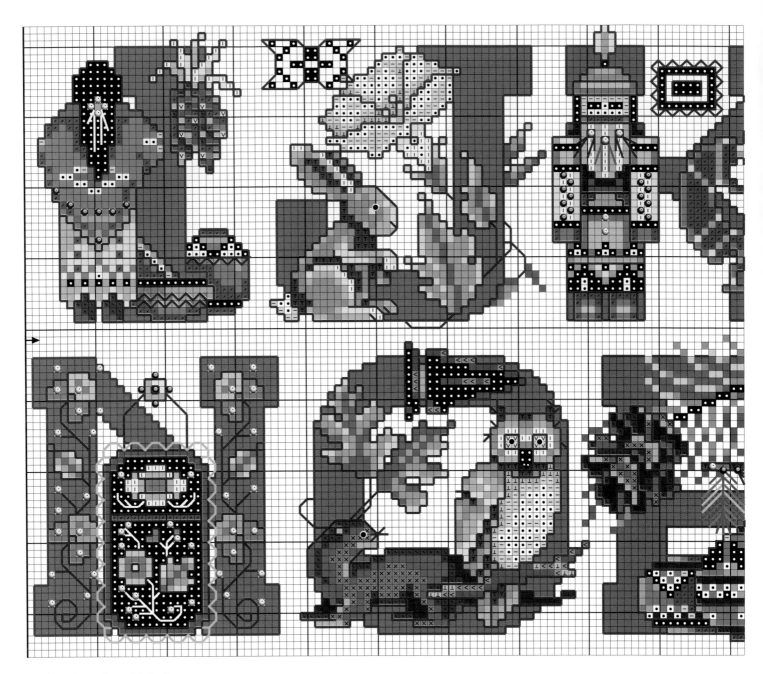

Native American Alphabet

DMC stranded cotton

Cross stitch

155	⊙ 356	436	729	3011	╱ 3826
◼ 310	367	597	╲ 801	3746	3829
⊲ 317	368	598	T 869	Z 3747	3830
⊥ 318	− 415	676	938	3755	• blanc
320	434	I 677	976	3777	
322	✕ 435	V 726	977	3799	Kreinik #4 102 vatican

Backstitch/Long stitch

— 310	— 3755
— 322	— 3829
— 801	▭ blanc
— 934	Kreinik 102
— 3746	

French knots

● 310

Mill Hill beads

◉ 10004 jet
◉ 10028 silver

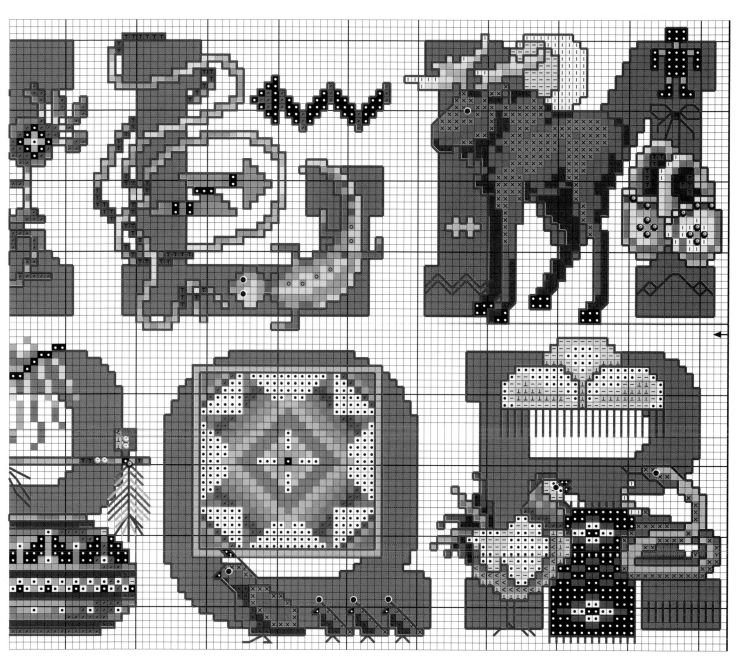

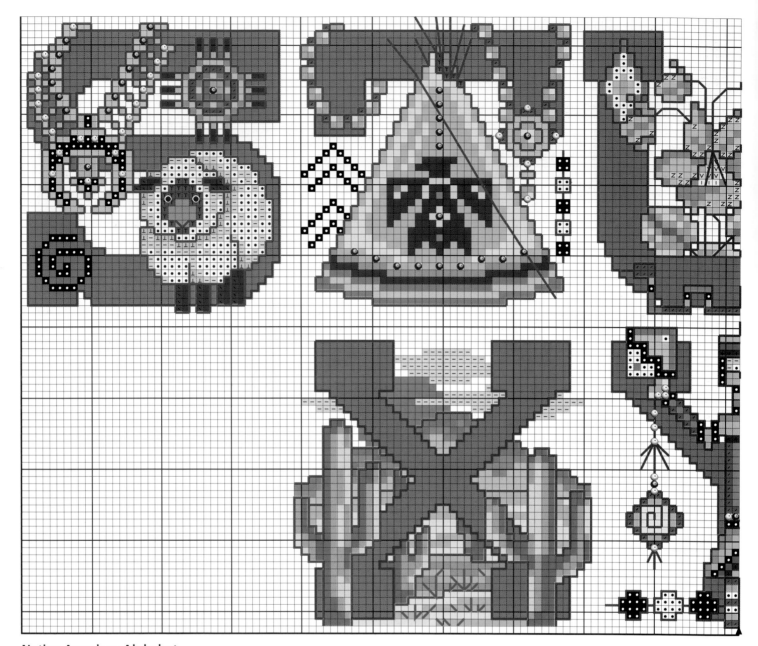

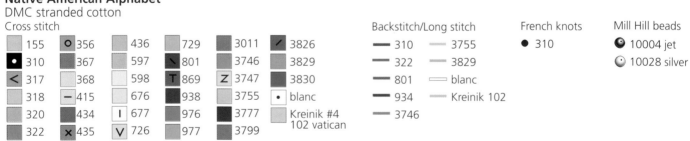

Native American Alphabet
DMC stranded cotton
Cross stitch

155	O 356	436	729	3011	/ 3826	
310	367	597	\ 801	3746	3829	
< 317	368	598	T 869	Z 3747	3830	
318	− 415	676	938	3755	3830	
320	434	I 677	976	3777	· blanc	
322	× 435	V 726	977	3799	Kreinik #4 102 vatican	

Backstitch/Long stitch

— 310	— 3755
— 322	— 3829
— 801	— blanc
— 934	— Kreinik 102
— 3746	

French knots

● 310

Mill Hill beads

◉ 10004 jet
◎ 10028 silver

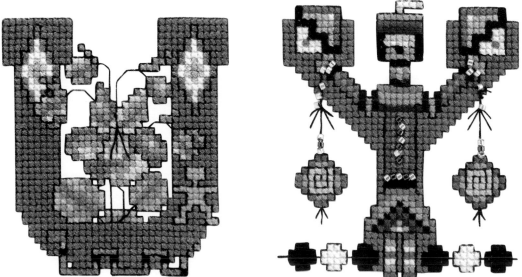

Navajo Sewing Collection

When you have talent of any kind,
Use it, guard it, take care of it
(Sauk)

Seated before her large outdoor loom, the Navajo weaver creates what most would consider a work of art. Behind its practical application the rug she works on carries a rich tradition uniquely identifiable in the Navajo culture. History tells us that these people first acquired their sheep from the Spanish and learned weaving from the Pueblo peoples in the late 17th century, but Navajo legend has it that Spider Woman was the spirit being who came from the canyons to teach the women this traditional craft.

In hand-woven baskets, the weaver gathers her hanks of yarn, hand-spun and dyed with native plants. Around her shoulders she wears a wool blanket woven in a classic red, white and black pattern. With patience and artistry, her masterpiece unfolds.

Your sewing supplies will be wonderfully close at hand in a Nantucket sewing basket, the original form of which was introduced to New England lightship keepers by the local American Indians. The dazzling finished rug pattern with its pure colours is repeated in a handy pincushion and matching needle case, each with an extra touch of beading to add to their elegance. For a special treat, make up a small scissors fob so you will never again misplace your favourite pair of scissors.

➤ A jewel-toned scissors fob, pincushion and needle case adorned with sparkling cranberry and opal beads are quick to stitch and make very pretty tokens for a stitching friend.

Materials

- 30.5 x 30.5cm (12 x 12in) natural 14-count Aida
- Tapestry needle size 24 and a beading needle
- DMC stranded cotton (floss) as listed in chart key
- Mill Hill Magnifica™ glass beads: 10079 brilliant teal and 10089 true silver
- 20.3cm (8in) diameter Nantucket basket with matching 18cm (7in) lid (see Suppliers)
- 18cm (7in) square of Ultrasuede® to tone with embroidery
- 61cm (24in) length of leather cord to tone with embroidery
- Permanent fabric glue

Stitch count 95h x 95w
Design size 17 x 17cm
(6¾ x 6¾in)

Nantucket Sewing Basket

1 Prepare for work, referring to page 100 if necessary. Mark the centre of the fabric and chart (page 70). For your own use you could enlarge the chart on a colour photocopier. Mount your fabric in an embroidery frame if you wish.

2 Start stitching from the centre of the chart, using two strands of stranded cotton (floss) for cross stitches and one strand for the black backstitch (shown in dark blue/grey on the chart for clarity). Use one strand for French knots, winding the thread twice around the needle. Using a beading needle and matching thread, attach the beads (see page 102) in the positions shown on the chart.

3 One all stitching is complete follow the manufacturer's instructions for mounting your embroidery on the basket lid. Cut a circle of Ultrasuede® to cover the back of the lid. To make the lifting tabs for the lid, cut two 1.25 x 15.2cm (½ x 6in) strips from the remaining scraps of Ultrasuede®. Fold each strip in half and, with the raw ends pointing towards the centre back of the lid and 2.5cm (1in) showing above the lid top, glue the strips at the centre of opposite sides.

4 Run a thin line of fabric glue all around halfway down the sides of the lid cushion. Attach the leather cord, starting and ending at centre bottom and gluing cut edges together. Glue on the circle of Ultrasuede® to cover the back of the lid and all raw edges.

Navajo Pincushion

Stitch a useful pincushion on a 20.3cm (8in) square of natural 14-count Aida, following the chart on page 71 and the stitching instructions above. Cut iron-on interfacing 2.5cm (1in) larger than the finished embroidery and press on to the wrong side. Trim the embroidery leaving twelve rows beyond the edge. Pin a square of backing fabric and the trimmed embroidery right sides together. Stitch a 1.25cm (½in) seam all round using the fabric weave as a guide and leaving an opening for turning at the bottom. Turn to the right side and stuff with polyester filling. Using permanent fabric glue or slipstitching, attach a decorative trim around the edges, beginning and ending at centre bottom. Tuck in the braid ends at the opening and slipstitch closed. Attach a decorative button at the bottom to finish.

Stitch count 47h x 47w
Design size 8.5 x 8.5cm (3⅜ x 3⅜in)

Materials

(for needle case and fob)

- Two pieces 18 x 18cm (7 x 7in) natural 18-count Aida

- Tapestry needle size 24 and a beading needle

- DMC stranded cotton (floss) as listed in chart key

- Mill Hill Magnifica™ glass beads: 10046 white opal and 10033 antique cranberry

- Three co-ordinating pieces of felt 9 x 18cm (3½ x 7in) for needle case

- Iron-on interfacing 9 x 15.2cm (3½ x 6in) for needle case

- Fusible web for needle case (see Suppliers)

- Two 15.24cm (6in) lengths of ribbon to tone with embroidery for needle case

- One decorative button for needle case

- Permanent fabric glue

- 18cm (7in) hanging cord to tone with embroidery for fob

Stitch count (for each project)
41h x 41w
Design size (for each project)
5.8 x 5.8cm (2¼ x 2¼in)

Needle Case and Scissors Fob

1 Follow steps 1 and 2 of the sewing basket for stitching the design, using the chart on page 71 (the same design is used for the needle case and fob).

Making Up a Needle Case

2 Cut iron-on interfacing 2.5cm (1in) larger than the finished embroidery and press on the wrong side. Trim to within eight rows of the embroidery.

3 Prepare the case by layering felt, fusible web (cut to make sure it doesn't overlap the felt edges) and another piece of felt on top. Press to fuse the layers. Cut the remaining piece of felt into two 7.6cm (3in) squares. Fold the case in half and crease. Pink the edges and the two felt squares. Open the case and place the ends of each ribbon at the centres of the shorter sides, 1.25cm (½in) in from the edge. Cut two pieces of fusible web to fit behind the felt squares (not peeking beyond the edges). Centre each felt square with a layer of web beneath on either side of the crease on the inside of the case, making sure to catch the ribbon ends. Press and fuse securely. Fold the finished case in half and tie the ribbons in a bow.

4 Cut fusible web to fit behind the embroidery. Centre the embroidery with the web beneath on the front of the case and press to fuse. With fabric glue, attach the decorative cord all around the edge of the embroidery, beginning and ending at the centre right side. Attach a decorative button where the ends meet.

Making Up a Scissors Fob

1 Trim the Aida to within 1.25cm (½in) of the embroidery. Cut a piece of Aida the same size. Using one strand of black stranded cotton (floss), stitch a running stitch one row beyond the last row of the embroidery, making the fob 42 x 42 stitches. Repeat this running stitch around a 42 x 42 stitch area on the blank Aida.

2 Trim both pieces of Aida to within four rows of the running stitch and fold along this line of stitches. Finger press in place, mitring corners. Secure the cord and tassel to the back. With wrong sides together, use two strands of black thread to whip stitch the running backstitches from both pieces, starting at centre bottom. Tuck in the ends of the hanging cord at centre top as you go. Cut eight 7.6cm (3in) lengths of six-stranded black cotton. Tie the ends in a knot and tuck the knotted end in at centre bottom. Stuff with polyester filling and finish whip stitching until all edges are sealed. Decorate the tassels with beads.

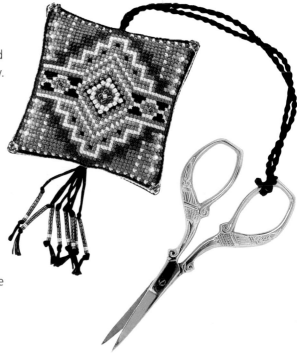

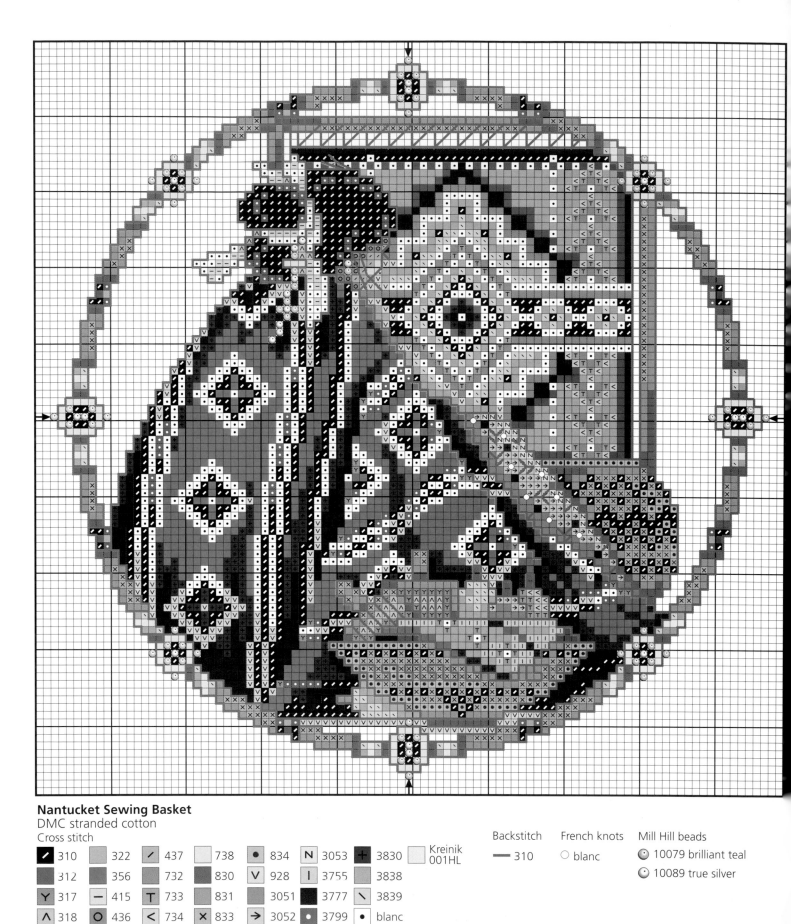

Nantucket Sewing Basket
DMC stranded cotton
Cross stitch

◤ 310	322	╱ 437	738	• 834	N 3053	✚ 3830	Kreinik 001HL		
312	356	732	830	V 928	I 3755	3838			
Y 317	— 415	T 733	831	3051	3777	╲ 3839			
∧ 318	O 436	< 734	✕ 833	→ 3052	3799	• blanc			

Backstitch
— 310

French knots
○ blanc

Mill Hill beads
◉ 10079 brilliant teal
◉ 10089 true silver

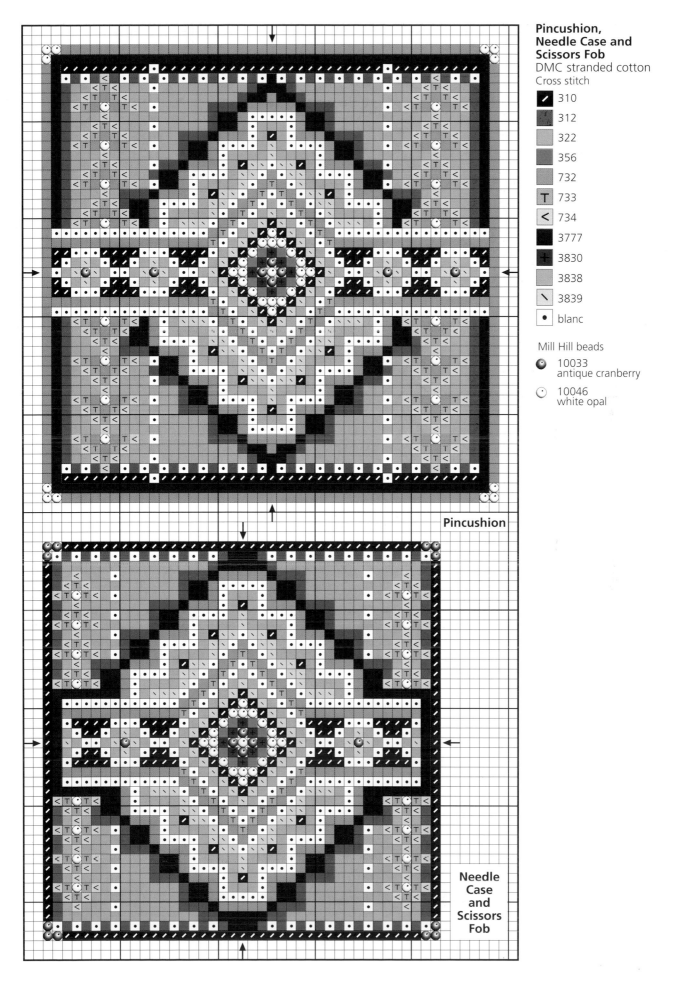

**Pincushion,
Needle Case and
Scissors Fob**
DMC stranded cotton
Cross stitch

/	310
	312
	322
	356
	732
T	733
<	734
	3777
+	3830
	3838
\	3839
•	blanc

Mill Hill beads

10033
antique cranberry

10046
white opal

Pincushion

**Needle
Case
and
Scissors
Fob**

The Circle of Life

All dreams spin out from the same web
(Hopi)

Native Americans myths and stories are filled with the ancient symbolizm of the circle. This holy sign signifies strength, spirituality, and unity. Holding the infinite cycle of life and the four sacred powers of the universe, the circle was used to watch over and guide every aspect of native life.

Dream catchers were used for protection during the quiet darkness of the night. At the centre of the sinew web, bad dreams were captured and kept from touching the sleeper so that in the early morning sunlight they would evaporate with the dew. Beneficial dreams were caught on the delicate feathers and beads, softly drifting down to ensure the dreamer's safe keeping.

With a border of morning stars guiding the way and two turquoise bear fetishes to bring strength, this magical ring, stitched in the delicate, muted colours of the earth and sky, celebrates the oneness of all our lives and the power of our hopes for the future.

Materials

- 51 x 43cm (20 x 17in)
  14-count Fiddler's Light Aida
- Tapestry needle size 24
- DMC stranded cotton (floss)
  as listed in chart key
- Kreinik #4 Very Fine Braid
  102HL vatican hi lustre

Stitch count 182h x 147w
Design size 33 x 26.7cm
(13 x 10½in)

Dream Catcher Picture

1 Prepare for work, referring to page 100 if necessary. Mark the centre of the fabric and the centre of the chart overleaf. Mount your fabric in an embroidery frame if you wish.

2 Start stitching from the centre of the chart. Use one strand of thread for Kreinik 102HL and DMC 642 cross stitches. Use two strands of stranded cotton (floss) for all other full and three-quarter cross stitches. Use one strand wrapped twice around the needle for French knots. Work the long stitches in the feathers with two strands. Please note: some long stitches are shown as dotted lines on the chart for clarity but should be stitched as full-length long stitches. Use two strands of white for the backstitches on the bear fetishes in the bottom border and one strand for all other backstitches.

3 Once all the stitching is complete, finish your picture by mounting and framing (see page 103).

Dream Catcher Picture
DMC stranded cotton
Cross stitch

Cross stitch							
△ 156	+ 334	597	I 746	⟋ 3013	⟍ 3746	Kreinik 102HL
⊡ 310	341	Y 598	Z 747	V 3045	− 3755	
312	✕ 368	L 640	⟋ 792	3046	3787	
320	420	642	3012	T 3047	• blanc	

Backstitch/Long stitch	
—— 156	—— 792
—— 310	- - - 3746
—— 312	—— 3755
••••• 334	—— blanc
—— 597	

French knots
● 310
● 3012

Dream Catcher Picture
DMC stranded cotton

Cross stitch

△ 156	+ 334	597	I 746	/ 3013	\ 3746	Kreinik 102HL
● 310	341	Y 598	Z 747	V 3045	– 3755	
312	× 368	L 640	/ 792	3046	3787	
320	420	642	3012	T 3047	● blanc	

Backstitch/Long stitch

156	792
310	3746
312	3755
334	blanc
597	

French knots

● 310
● 3012

Desert Flowers

*Listen to the voice of nature,
for it holds treasures for you*
(Huron)

Each spring all across the desert a strange and magical change takes place. From the first delicate violet blossoms of the sand verbena to sweeping summer hillsides of Arizona poppies, this seemingly desolate and barren landscape is miraculously transformed. After waiting long months for just the right amount of rain, an amazing array of colourful blooms unfold. The desert palette can be as varied as in any cottage garden. From the sweet pinks and mauves of the rock hibiscus, its lighter variation also known as 'paleface', to the deep violet blues of desert lupine, the earth yields to these once invisible treasures. Names such as Indian paintbrush, desert bells and Navajo clover pay homage to the habitats of these delightful wildflowers.

Native Americans use the bulb of the ajo lily, with its garlic-like taste, in cooking. The poisonous sacred datura, or Jimson weed, is used as a hallucinogenic substance in coming-of-age ceremonies, and the woody stems of blue flax are used in papermaking, while the seeds yield a highly nutritious oil. With beauty and purpose, the flowers of the desert at once surprise and enchant all that are lucky enough to catch their glorious display.

➤ A wonderful pillow edged with ornate braid is the perfect way to display the thirteen colourful desert flowers in this beautiful design. Any of the flower motifs could be singled out for smaller projects, such as the lovely album cover shown here.

Materials

- 33 x 66cm (13 x 26in) flax 14-count Aida (DMC code 738)
- Tapestry needle size 24
- DMC stranded cotton (floss) as listed in chart key
- Lightweight iron-on interfacing
- 0.5m (½yd) backing fabric
- Polyester filling
- 1.8m (2yd) decorative braid

Stitch count 115h x 295w
Design size 21 x 53.5cm (8¼ x 21in)

Desert Flowers Pillow

1 Prepare for work, referring to page 100 if necessary. Mark the centre of the fabric and chart (pages 82–85). Mount fabric in a frame if you wish.

2 Start stitching from the centre of the chart and fabric, using two strands of stranded cotton (floss) for full and three-quarter cross stitches. Following the chart for colour changes, work all French knots using one strand wrapped twice around the needle and work all backstitches using one strand.

Making Up a Pillow

1 Once all stitching is complete, make up into a pillow as follows. Start by trimming the embroidery, leaving fourteen rows beyond the edges all around. Cut a piece of iron-on interfacing to the same size and press on to the wrong side of the embroidery to fuse together, following the manufacturer's instructions.

2 Cut the backing fabric to the same size as the trimmed embroidery and pin in place, right sides facing. Using matching sewing thread, stitch a 1.25cm (½in) seam all around, leaving an opening at the bottom for turning through. Turn through to the right side and stuff with polyester filling. Slipstitch the bottom opening closed leaving a small gap at the centre bottom.

3 Slipstitch the decorative braid around all edges beginning at centre bottom. To finish tuck the ends into the small gap and slipstitch closed.

Rose Hibiscus Box

What a wonderful hostess gift this covered box would make. On graph paper, draw a rectangle covering 66 x 50 squares. Leaving at least two empty rows all around, add the inner three-square border from the main chart. Stitch the design on 28 x 23cm (11 x 9in) antique white 14-count Aida.

Purchase a covered box slightly larger than the finished embroidery. Trim the embroidery to within 1.25cm (½in) of the stitching and fold back the edges to the last row. Place cotton wadding (batting) or felt behind the embroidery so the box colour doesn't show. Glue the folded edges on the back, centre the embroidery on the box top and press down. Glue decorative cord around the folded edge, starting at the bottom, and attach a button to finish.

Stitch count of rose hibiscus 66h x 50w
Design size 12 x 9cm (4¾ x 3½in)

Lily Bag

To make up this small sachet bag you will need a 25.4 x 20.3cm (10 x 8in) piece of khaki 14-count Aida, two 25.4 x 20.3cm (10 x 8in) pieces of background/lining fabric to tone with the embroidery, 38cm (15in) length of 6mm (¼in) wide velvet ribbon and six decorative beads. Stitch the lily following the pillow instructions opposite.

Trim the finished embroidery 6.3cm (2½in) from the top of the stitching and 2.5cm (1in) from the bottom and both sides. Fold the top edge to the back by 1.25cm (½in) and press. Trim background fabric pieces to the size of the trimmed embroidery leaving an extra 5cm (2in) at the top. Aligning bottom and side edges, layer a piece of background fabric right side up, the trimmed embroidery right side up, and the second piece of background fabric wrong side up. Stitch a 1.25cm (½in) seam along the sides and bottom edge, leaving the top open. Turn the embroidery to the right side creating a lining and backing. Fold the two top flaps in to meet the folded edge of the embroidery and slipstitch the edge to one side of the lining. Fill with pot-pourri or a special trinket and tie with velvet ribbon trimmed with beads.

Stitch count of lily 49h x 46w
Design size 9 x 8.5cm (3½ x 3¼in)

Desert Bells Album

You can create a simple album cover using one of the paper albums now available. Here, the desert bells design is stitched on 18 x 18cm (7 x 7in) antique white 18-count Aida. You could work different butterflies if you like. Mount and decorate your finished embroidery like a card (see page 102). In this sample, the original ribbon tying the album has been changed to one that tones with the embroidery. A decorative edging of violet suede has been glued around the window with a small satin flower added at centre bottom to finish.

Stitch count of desert bells 36 x 36
Design size 5 x 5cm (2 x 2in)

Desert Flowers
DMC stranded cotton
Cross stitch

O	153
●	310
+	318
	340
	341
	349
→	351
/	415
	470
I	471
	472
	501
×	502
	503
	553
	554
	725
L	726
Y	727
V	741
−	746
←	762
N	816
\	818
	972
Z	3045
	3046
	3047
/	3371
✓	3687
T	3688
	3689
	3746
	3813
<	3853
	3857
•	blanc

Backstitch
— 3345
— 3371
— blanc

French knots
○ 727
● 3345
● 3371
● 3857
○ blanc

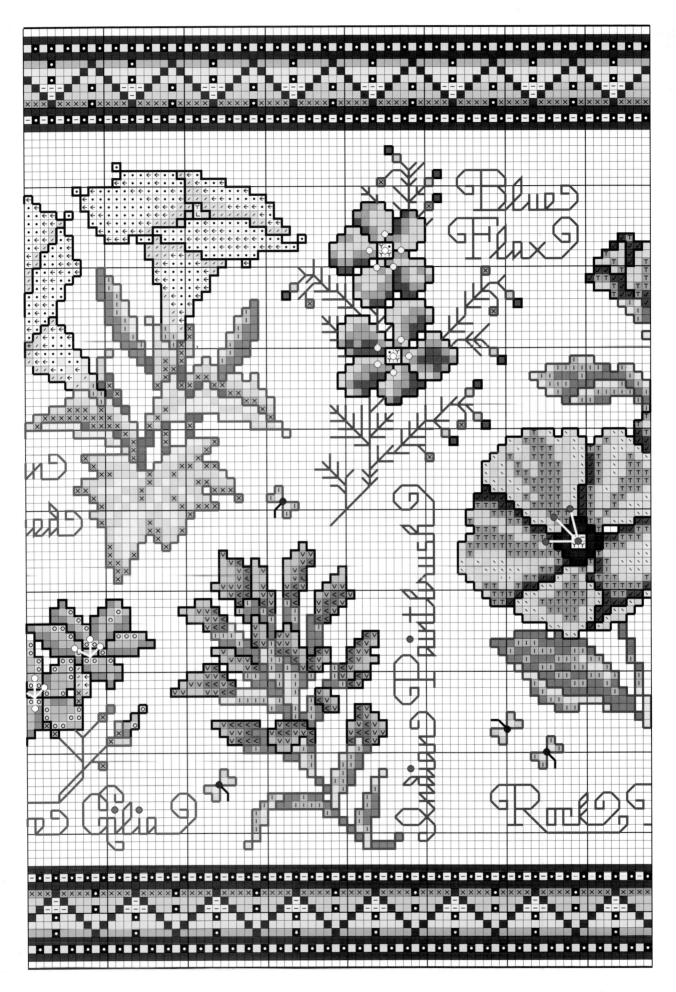

Desert Flowers
DMC stranded cotton
Cross stitch

○	153
◉	310
+	318
	340
	341
	349
→	351
/	415
	470
I	471
	472
	501
×	502
	503
	553
	554
	725
L	726
Y	727
V	741
–	746
←	762
N	816
\	818
	972
Z	3045
	3046
	3047
/	3371
✓	3687
T	3688
	3689
	3746
	3813
<	3853
	3857
•	blanc

Backstitch
— 3345
— 3371
═ blanc

French knots
○ 727
● 3345
● 3371
● 3857
○ blanc

Desert Flowers 85

Gifts of Wisdom

*The more you give,
the more good things come to you*
(Crow)

The practice of sharing and giving creates a true spiritual connection. Offering words of hope and celebration we give love and support to all of those close to us. For generations, Native Americans have handed down gifts of wise and gentle words to guide and encourage their people. With this collection of small projects you can pass this wisdom on to those you love.

These precious words to live by can be given as cards, made up into wall hangings or crafted into fragrant sachets and useful bags. Gleaming glass beads and metallic threads enhance the ethereal quality of each design. The messages speak of kindness, strength and the joy of the shining sun. They encourage us to be gentle, to walk with pride in ourselves and to be conscious of our place in the world. Suitable for almost any occasion, these gentle words are sure to bring light to all who receive them.

➤ This collection of meaningful sentiments will delight anyone who receives them. Their possibilities are open to your imagination and can be worked up as any of the projects presented here or use your creativity to make up your own pillows, sachet bags or album covers.

Be Kind to
Everything
That Lives

Live Strong
as the
Mountains

Walk Tall
as the
Trees

Be Known
by the
tracks you
leave

Be Gentle
as the
Spring Rain

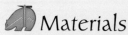

Materials

(for stitching each design)

- 20.3 x 17.8cm (8 x 7in) 18-count Rustico® Aida (Zweigart code 3292/154/51)
- Tapestry needle size 24 and a beading needle
- DMC stranded cotton (floss) as listed in chart key
- Kreinik Very Fine #4 Braid: 021HL copper hi lustre and 029 turquoise
- Mill Hill Magnifica™ glass beads: 10013 copper; 10028 silver and 10079 brilliant teal

Stitch count (each design)
57h x 43w
Design size 8 x 6cm (3⅛ x 2⅜in)

Gifts of Wisdom Cards

1 Prepare for work, referring to page 100 if necessary. Mark the centre of the fabric and chart (pages 91–93). Mount your fabric in an embroidery frame if you wish. Please note: a single key has been used for all six designs but you may not need all of the colours for every design.

2 Start stitching from the centre of the chart. Use one strand for all Kreinik cross stitches and two strands of stranded cotton (floss) for all other full

and three-quarter cross stitches. Work French knots with two strands wrapped once around the needle and backstitches with one strand. Using a beading needle and matching thread, attach the beads (see page 102).

3 Once all stitching is complete, mount your embroidery in a suitable card (see page 102 and also suggestions for decorating card mounts) or make up into a wall hanging, a bag or a sachet, as described below and opposite.

Making Up a Sachet

1 Place the two pieces of felt back to back. Stitch a 2.5cm (1in) seam all around, leaving a gap for stuffing.

Materials

- Two pieces of 15.2 x 14cm (6 x 5½in) felt to tone with embroidery
- One strip 35.5 x 6mm (14 x ¼in) felt for hanging cord
- 40.64cm (16in) length of braided leather trim
- Lightweight iron-on interfacing
- Fusible web (see Suppliers)
- Polyester stuffing and pot-pourri (optional)
- Four decorative beads
- One decorative button
- Permanent fabric glue

2 Cut lightweight interfacing to the same size as the embroidery and fuse it to the wrong side of the embroidery. Trim the finished embroidery to within seven rows of the border edge. Cut a piece of fusible web to the same size and place it on the wrong side of the embroidery making sure the edges do not overlap the trimmed embroidery.

3 Centre the finished embroidery with the fusible web beneath within the stitching lines on the sachet and press to fuse. Pink all four edges of the felt with pinking shears and clip with sharp scissors to just before the stitching lines to create a fringe. Stuff the sachet with polyester stuffing and pot-pourri. Close the opening with machine stitching. Glue the braided trim around the raw edge of the embroidery starting and ending at centre bottom, attaching a decorative button at the cut ends. Create a hanger by tacking (basting) the hanging cord to the upper corners of the sachet at the stitching line, leaving 5cm (2in) hanging. Add decorative beads as desired.

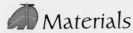 Materials

- Ultrasuede® : 53.3 x 16.5cm (21 x 6½in) for backing; 23 x 30.5cm (9 x 12in) for contrasting border and four 76cm x 6mm (30 x ¼in) lengths for hanging cord
- Lightweight iron-on interfacing
- Fusible web (see Suppliers)
- Assorted feathers and beads
- Twelve decorative buttons
- 23cm (9in) wooden dowel 6mm (¼in) diameter
- Permanent fabric glue

Making Up a Wall Hanging

1 Using pinking shears trim the 53.3 x 16.5cm (21 x 6½in) Ultrasuede® background fabric close to all four edges. To create a casing for the dowel, with the fabric positioned vertically, turn the top edge to the back by 2.5cm (1in) and glue carefully close to the pinked edge. To create the bottom fringe, draw a line on the back of the fabric 2.5cm (1in) from the bottom edge. With sharp scissors, cut the fringe to this line, using the pinked indentations as a guide.

2 Cut three pieces of lightweight interfacing the same size as the three embroideries and fuse to the wrong sides following the manufacturer's instructions. Trim the finished embroideries to within seven rows of the border edges. Cut pieces of fusible web the same size and place on the wrong side of each embroidery making sure the edges do not overlap the trimmed embroidery. Centre the first of the three embroideries on the fabric between the top folded edge and the bottom of the fringed edge. Now, place the other embroideries above and below the centre design leaving approximately 5.7cm (2¼in) from the top and bottom edges of the background fabric. When all designs are evenly spaced, press to fuse the embroidery and background fabric together.

3 Cut twelve 12.7 x 1cm (5 x ⅜in) lengths of Ultrasuede® contrasting border fabric and place around each embroidery leaving four rows of Aida showing. Trim as necessary and carefully glue down with fabric glue. Glue a decorative button at each corner.

4 Insert the dowel through the top casing. Attach the hanging cord by tying a knot around each dowel end, leaving at least 17.8cm (7in) of cord hanging on each side. Add two additional cords to each side if you like and thread beads and feathers on the ends. A dab of fabric glue at the feather ends will prevent them from slipping out of the beads.

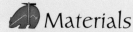 Materials

- Two pieces 26.6 x 12.7cm (10½ x 5in) Ultrasuede®
- 91cm (36in) length of toning suede cord
- Lightweight iron-on interfacing
- Fusible web (see Suppliers)
- Assorted beads
- One decorative button
- Permanent fabric glue

Making Up a Bag

1 Trim the finished embroidery to within eight rows of the border edge. Using a neutral sewing thread to blend with the Aida, run a machine stitch three rows beyond the embroidery. Remove the Aida threads up to the machine stitching to create a fringe.

2 Cut a piece of lightweight interfacing the size of the trimmed embroidery (excluding the fringe) and fuse it to the wrong side following the manufacturer's instructions. Cut a piece of fusible web the same size and place on the wrong side of the embroidery making sure the edges do not overlap the fringe.

3 Holding one piece of Ultrasuede® vertically, on the wrong side draw a line 5cm (2in) from the bottom edge. Fold over the top edge to the wrong side by 2cm (¾in) and press. Align the bottom edge of the second piece with the drawn line on the first, wrong sides facing. Tack (baste) to hold in place. Using the edge of the second piece of

Ultrasuede® as your guide, stitch a 1.25cm (½in) seam across the bottom and up the two sides, leaving the top edge free. This will leave a 5cm (2in) piece of fabric free at the top for the closing flap and at the bottom for the fringe. Pink all four edges. Using the pinking notches as a guide carefully cut the fabric to create a fringe, stopping just before the bottom stitching line. On the front side of the bag, place a button

at the centre 2cm (¾in) from the folded edge. Turn the top flap to the front and, locating the sewn button, cut a slit in the fabric to pass it through for closing. To attach a carrying cord, glue the length of suede cord along the fold on the back piece of fabric. Attach decorative beads to your liking.

4 To attach the embroidery to the bag front, with the bag closed, centre the embroidery with the fusible web beneath, taking care not to overlap the fringe, and then press to fuse.

Gifts of Wisdom
DMC sranded cotton
Cross stitch

✓	156			
▮	322			
⌄	334			
N	340			
⌄	434			

	470			
⊤	471			
	472			
●	500			
▬	501			

	502		▬	801
⁄	597		+	818
	598		↓	976
⌐	747			977
	761			986

⊤	987		Y	3852
	989		•	blanc
	3371			Kreinik 021HL
⁄	3747			Kreinik 029
⌐	3755			

Z	3810		
⌐	3821		
	3822		
O	3826		
	3841		

Backstitch
— 156
— 501
— 801
— 986
— 3371
— 3810

French knots
○ 761
● 3371

Mill Hill beads
○ 10013 copper
○ 10028 silver
○ 10079 teal

Live Strong
as the
Mountains

Be Gentle
as the
Spring Rain

Gifts of Wisdom

DMC stranded cotton

Cross stitch

✓ 156	502	T 987	Y 3852
⊤ 322	╱ 597	989	• blanc
V 334	598	◢ 3371	Kreinik 021HL
N 340	L 747	I 801	◢ 3810	● 3821	Kreinik 029
⊙ 500	761	+ 818	Z 3810	I 3821
Y 501		↓ 976	< 3747	3822
		977	× 3755	○ 3826
		986		3841
✓ 470			
⊤ 471			
V 472			
⊙ 500			
I 501			
Y 434			

Backstitch

— 156
— 501
— 801
— 986
— 3371
— 3810

French knots

⊙ 761
● 3371

Mill Hill beads

⊙ 10013 copper
⊙ 10028 silver
⊙ 10079 teal

Indian Warrior

You already possess everything to become great
(Crow)

With distant gaze and proud determination, an Indian warrior stands tall before the challenge he faces. A specially woven robe drapes his broad shoulders and enfolds him in a gesture of warmth and protection, its red colour a symbol of success and triumph.

The young brave is dressed in fringed and beaded buckskin leggings and shirt, his chest protected by an elaborate breastplate of pipe bones and beads in turquoise, jet and copper.

In his strong hands he grasps a war lance covered in strips of buffalo hide decorated with silver amulets and trimmed with ermine. In the crook of his arm rests a pipe tomahawk used to negotiate both war and peace. A glistening moon surrounds him with sacred symbols of wisdom and vision to guide his way. In time, the warrior will prove his skill in battle and earn the prized eagle feathers whose spirit will continue to protect him in all his endeavours.

Materials

- 58 x 48cm (23 x 19in) oatmeal 28-count evenweave
- Tapestry needle size 24 and a beading needle
- DMC stranded cotton (floss) as listed in chart key
- Kreinik #4 Very Fine Braid: 001 silver (2 spools); 032 pearl (3 spools) and 194 pale blue (1 spool)
- Mill Hill Magnifica™ glass beads: 10004 jet; 10079 brilliant teal; 10080 brilliant bronze and 10089 true silver

Stitch count 243h x 187w
Design size 44 x 34cm
(17½ x 13½in)

1 Prepare for work, referring to page 100 if necessary. Mark the centre of the fabric and centre of the chart overleaf. Mount your fabric in an embroidery frame if you wish.

2 Following the chart for colour changes, use two strands for the long stitches in the blue feathers near the head and on the blue and brown feathers on the quiver at centre left. Use one strand to stitch all Kreinik thread cross stitches, long stitches and backstitches. Work all other long stitches and backstitches using one strand of stranded cotton (floss). Using a beading needle and matching thread, attach the beads (see page 102) following the colour changes on the chart.

3 Once all the stitching is complete, finish your picture by mounting and framing (see page 103).

Indian Warrior
DMC stranded cotton
Cross stitch

● 310	\ 322	◉ 400	435	597	I 733	O 3022	3045	3743	V 3776	3799
∧ 317	356	← 415	╱ 436	T 598	− 738	3023	⊥ 3046	3753	3777	3830
Z 318	367	N 434	437	732	869	3042	3047	3755	─ 3787	● blanc

Kreinik #4 Braid

	001 silver
	032 pearl
L	194 pale blue

96 *Indian Warrior*

Backstitch/Long stitch

— 310 — 436 — 3746
— 322 — 732 — 3755
— 400 — 869 — Kreinik 001
— 434 — 3045

Mill Hill beads

◉ 10004 jet ◉ 10080 bronze

◉ 10079 teal ◉ 10089 silver

Indian Warrior
DMC stranded cotton
Cross stitch

Kreinik #4 Braid

◼	310	◥	322	◉	400		435		597	I	733	○	3022		3045		3743	V	3776		3799		001 silver
∧	317		356	←	415	∕	436	T	598	−	738		3023	⊥	3046		3753	◼	3777		3830		032 pearl
Z	318		367	N	434		437		732		869		3042		3047		3755	−	3787	•	blanc	L	194 pale blue

Backstitch/Long stitch
— 310   — 436   — 3746
— 322   — 732   — 3755
— 400   — 869   — Kreinik 001
— 434   — 3045

Mill Hill beads
● 10004 jet   ◐ 10080 bronze
◐ 10079 teal   ◐ 10089 silver

Materials, Techniques and Making Up

This brief section describes the materials and equipment required, the basic techniques used and some general making up methods. Refer to Suppliers for useful addresses.

Materials

Very few materials are required for cross stitch embroidery, although many of the projects in this book have been given an authentic feel by embellishment with feathers and beads.

Fabrics

The designs have been worked predominantly on a blockweave fabric called Aida. If you change the gauge (count) of the material, that is the number of holes per inch, then the size of the finished work will alter accordingly. The designs could also be stitched on an evenweave such as linen but will need to be worked over two fabric threads instead of one block.

Threads

The projects have been stitched with DMC stranded embroidery cotton (floss) but you could match the colours to other thread ranges – ask in your local needlecraft shop for information or refer to Suppliers on page 104 for Anchor and Madeira thread details. The six-stranded skeins can easily be split into separate threads. The project instructions tell you how many strands to use.

Needles

Tapestry needles, available in different sizes, are used for cross stitch as they have a rounded point and do not snag fabric. A thinner beading needle will be needed to attach seed beads.

Frames

Whether you use an embroidery frame to keep your fabric taut while stitching is a matter of personal preference. Generally speaking, working with a frame helps to keep the tension even and prevent distortion, while working without a frame is faster and less cumbersome. There are various types of frame on the market – ask for advice in your local needlecraft shop.

Techniques

Cross stitch embroidery requires few complicated techniques but your stitching will look its best if you follow the simple guidelines here.

Preparing the Fabric

Before starting work, check the design size given with each project and make sure that this tallies with the size that you require for your finished embroidery. Your fabric should be at least 5cm (2in) larger all the way round than the finished size of the stitching, to allow for making up. Before beginning to stitch, neaten the edges of the fabric either by hemming or zigzag stitching to stop the fabric fraying as you work.

Finding the Fabric Centre

Marking the centre of the fabric is important, regardless of which direction you work from, in order to stitch the design centrally on the fabric. To find the centre, fold the fabric in half horizontally and then vertically, then tack (baste) along the folds (or use tailor's chalk). The centre point is where the two lines of tacking (basting) meet. This point on the fabric should correspond to the centre point on the chart. Remove these lines on completion of the work.

Calculating Design Size

Each project in this book gives the stitch count and finished design size but if you want to work the design on a different count fabric the finished size will change and you will need to re-calculate the finished size. Divide the numbers of stitches in the design by the fabric count number, e.g., $140 \times 140 \div 14\text{-count} =$ a design size of $10 \times 10\text{in}$ ($25.5 \times 25.5\text{cm}$). Working on evenweave usually means working over two threads, so divide the count by two before you start calculating.

Using Charts and Keys

The charts in this book are easy to work from. Each square on the chart represents one stitch. Each coloured square, or coloured square with a symbol, represents a thread colour,

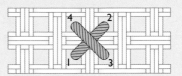

with the code number given in the chart key. A few of the designs use fractional stitches (three-quarter cross stitches) to give more definition to the design. Solid coloured lines show where backstitches or long stitches are to be worked. French knots are shown by coloured circles. Larger coloured circles with a dot indicate beads.

Each complete chart has arrows at the side to show the centre point, which you could mark with a pen. Where the charts have been split over several pages, the key is repeated. For your own use, you could colour photocopy and enlarge charts, taping the parts together.

Starting and Finishing Stitching

Avoid using knots when starting and finishing as this will make your work lumpy when mounted. Instead, bring the needle up at the start of the first stitch, leaving a 'tail' of about 2.5cm (1in) at the back. Secure the tail by working the first few stitches over it. Start new threads by first passing the needle through several stitches on the back of the work.

To finish off thread, pass the needle through some nearby stitches on the wrong side of the work, then cut the thread off close to the fabric.

Washing and Pressing

If you find it necessary to wash your finished embroidery, first make sure it is colourfast. Reds, dark blues and bright colours may be of special concern. Before using, wash the stranded cotton (floss) in tepid water and mild soap. Rinse well and then lay out flat to dry completely before stitching. Wash completed embroideries in the same way.

To iron work, use a medium setting and cover the ironing board with a thick layer of towelling. Place the stitching right side down and press gently.

The Stitches

Backstitch

Backstitches are used to give definition to and outline parts of a design. Many of the charts used different coloured backstitches. Follow Fig 1, bringing the needle up at 1 and down at 2, up at 3, down at 4 and so on.

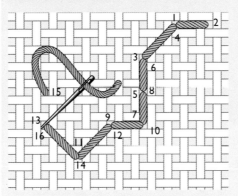

Fig 1 Backstitch (over two linen threads)

Cross Stitch

A cross stitch can be worked singly (Fig 2a) or a number of half stitches can be sewn in a line and completed on the return journey (Fig 2b).

To make a cross stitch over one block of Aida, bring the needle up through the fabric at the bottom left side of the stitch (number 1 on Fig 2a) and cross diagonally to the top right corner (2). Push the needle through the hole and bring up through the bottom right corner (3), crossing the fabric diagonally to the top left corner to finish the stitch (4). To work the next stitch, come up through the bottom right corner of the first stitch and repeat the steps above.

To work a row of cross stitches, stitch the first part of the stitch as above and repeat these half cross stitches along the row. Complete the crosses on the way back. Note: always finish the cross stitch with the top stitches lying in the same diagonal direction.

Fig 2a A single cross stitch on Aida

Fig 2b Working cross stitch in rows

French Knot

French knots have been used as eye highlights and details in some of the designs, in various colours. To work, follow Fig 3, bringing the needle and thread up through the fabric at the exact place where the knot is to be positioned. Wrap the thread once or twice around the needle (according to project instructions), holding the thread firmly close to the needle, then twist the needle back through the fabric as close as possible to where it first emerged. Holding the knot down, pull the thread through to the back leaving the knot on the surface, securing it with a small stitch on the back.

Fig 3 French knot

Long Stitch

This is used for the feathers in some of pictures. Simply work a long, straight stitch starting and finishing at the points indicated on the chart.

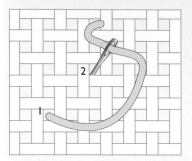

Fig 4 Long stitch

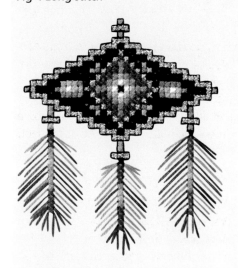

Three-quarter Cross Stitch

Three-quarter cross stitches give more detail to a design and can create the illusion of curves. They are shown by a triangle within a square on the charts. To work a three-quarter cross stitch, make a quarter stitch from the corner into the centre of the Aida square, piercing the fabric, and then work a half stitch across the other diagonal (Fig 5).

Fig 5 Three-quarter cross stitch

Attaching Beads

Adding beads will bring sparkle and texture to a cross stitch embroidery and are a feature of Native American design. Attach seed beads using ordinary sewing thread that matches the fabric colour and a beading needle or very fine 'sharp' needle and a half or whole cross stitch (Fig 6).

Fig 6 Attaching beads

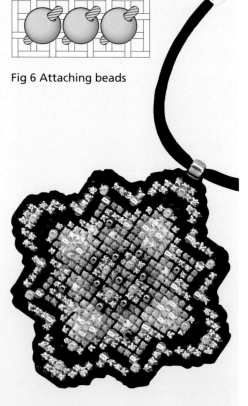

Making Up

The embroideries in this book are very versatile and can be made up in many ways. Generally, making up is included with projects but three general techniques are described here.

Making up into a Card

Many of the designs or parts of larger designs can be stitched and made up into cards. You will need: a ready-made card mount (aperture to fit embroidery) and craft glue or double-sided tape.

Trim the edges of the embroidery so it is slightly larger than the card aperture. Apply a thin coat of glue or a piece of double-sided tape to the inside of the card opening. Position the embroidery, checking that the stitching is central, and press down firmly. Fold the spare flap inside, sticking in place with glue or tape, and leave to dry before closing.

You can easily add a personal touch to ready-made card mounts by gluing on ribbons, bows, beads, buttons, stickers and even personal doodles in waterproof markers. Visit your local stationery or craft store and explore all the possibilities.

Making Up a Covered Album

These are general instructions for creating your own fabric-covered albums like the small photo album shown on page 40 of the Baby Blessings chapter.

 Materials

- One three-ring photo album sized to suit your project
- 0.5m (½yd) fabric for outside cover to tone with embroidery
- 0.5m (½yd) fabric for inside covers to tone with embroidery
- 0.5m (½yd) white cotton wadding (batting) or felt
- Two 25 x 30cm (10 x 12in) pieces heavy white card
- 1m (1yd) decorative cording to tone with embroidery
- 0.5m (½yd) decorative 1cm (³/₈in) ribbon to tone with embroidery
- Spray glue and permanent fabric glue
- One decorative button

1 Measure the inside cover of the album to the fold just before the metal spine. Cut two pieces of heavy card to the measurements, less 1.25cm (½in). Open the binder and lay it flat on the wadding (batting) or felt. Trace the outline of the album on to the batting or felt and cut out. In a well-ventilated area, spray one outside cover of the album with spray glue. Attach the batting or felt and repeat the process for the spine and back cover. Do not pull the felt over the cover too tightly, to ensure that the album will close. Trim the edges flush.

2 Lay the open album on the outer cover fabric. Measure and mark 5cm (2in) from all edges and cut the fabric. From the same fabric, cut two strips measuring the length of the metal spine plus 7.5cm (3in) wide. Fold over 6mm (¼in) on one long edge of each strip and press. Spray glue on the back of each strip and slide the folded edge under each side of the metal spine. You can use a butter knife to help push the edge beneath the spine.

3 Using the fabric for the inside cover, cut two pieces 1.25cm (½in) larger than the card. Spray glue on one side of each piece of the cut card. Place the fabric on the glued card leaving 1.25cm (½in) of fabric all around. Turn the edges to the back of the card and glue with permanent fabric glue.

4 Centre the open album on the outside cover fabric. Turn all the edges to the inside and glue, starting with the centre of each edge, leaving the corners and 7.5cm (3in) from the spine free. Carefully ease the corners to fit, and glue. At the top and bottom edges by the spine measure the fabric 1.25cm (½in) away from the fold in the album on each side of the metal spine and clip within 1.25cm (½in) of the top edge. Fold the fabric under between the two cuts and tuck the folded edge behind the top edge of the metal spine.

5 To assemble the album, cut the ribbon in half and centre one piece on each opening edge of the album at least 5cm (2in) in towards the centre. Glue the back of the covered card. Centre and attach this to the inside covers making sure the fold on the inside is free for closing.

6 Centre and glue the embroidery on the cover, taking care that no glue oozes out from the sides. Draw a thin bead of fabric glue around the edge of the embroidery starting and ending at centre bottom and attach decorative edging. Glue on a decorative button where the ends meet.

Making up as a Framed Picture

Many of the designs in this book make wonderful framed pictures. You will need: a picture frame (aperture size to fit embroidery); a piece of plywood or heavyweight card slightly smaller than the frame and wide adhesive tape or a staple gun.

Iron your embroidery and trim the edges if necessary, then centre the embroidery on the plywood or thick card. Fold the edges of the embroidery to the back and use adhesive tape or staples to fix in place. Insert the picture into the frame and secure with adhesive tape or staples. For a polished finish, with a wider choice of mounts and frames, take your work to a professional framer.

Suppliers

Charles Craft Inc
PO Box 1049, Laurenburg, NC 28353, USA
tel: 910 844 3521
email: ccraft@carolina.net
www.charlescraft.com
For fabrics for cross stitch and many useful pre-finished items (Coats Crafts UK supply some Charles Craft products in the UK)
Cot blanket: Babysoft™ Afghan fabric code AF 7311-0322
Bibs: blue gingham code BB-3650-4610 and ABC code BB-3650-1290
Place mats: Royal Classic country 14-count oatmeal code RC-4851-5452-PK
Napkins: Royal Classic country 14-count oatmeal napkins code RC-4852-5452-PK
Napkin rings: E-Z Stitch 14-count tan vinyl Aida code VC-2022-1639-PK
Towel: white 14-count Royal Classic velour code VT-6900-6750
Table runner: white 14-count Royal Classic code RC-4865-67450
Alphabet sachet: tea-dyed 28-count Monaco evenweave code EW-02326-6147

Coats Crafts UK
PO Box 22, Lingfield Estate, McMullen Road, Darlington, County Durham DL1 1YQ, UK
tel: 01325 365457 (for a list of stockists)
For Anchor stranded cotton (floss) and other embroidery supplies. Coats also supplies some Charles Craft products

Design Works Crafts Inc.
170 Wilbur Place, Bohemia, New York 11716, USA
tel: 631 244 5749
fax: 631 244 6138
email: customerservice@designworkscrafts.com
For cross stitch kits of Joan Elliott designs and for card mounts outside the UK

DMC Creative World
Pullman Road, Wigston, Leicestershire LE18 2DY, UK
tel: 0116 281 1040
fax: 0116 281 3592
www.dmc/cw.com
For stranded cotton (floss) and other embroidery supplies

Joan Elliott
www.joanelliottdesign.com

Framecraft Miniatures Ltd
Unit 3, Isis House, Linden Road, Brownhills, Walsall, West Midlands WS8 6LH, UK
tel: 01543 373 076
fax: 01543 453 154
www.framecraft.com
For wooden trinket bowls and boxes, notebook covers, pincushions, and many other pre-finished items with cross stitch inserts (trinket bowl code W3E)

Mill Hill, a division of Wichelt Imports Inc.
N162 Hwy 35, Stoddard WI 54658, USA
tel: 608 788 4600
fax: 608 788 6040
email: millhill@millhill.com
www.millhill.com
For Mill Hill beads and a US source for Framecraft products

Kreinik Manufacturing Company, Inc
3106 Timanus Lane, Suite 101, Baltimore, MD 21244, USA
tel: 1800 537 2166
email: kreinik@kreinik.com
www.kreinik.com
For a wide range of metallic threads and blending filaments

Madeira Threads (UK) Ltd
PO Box 6, Thirsk, North Yorkshire YO7 3YX, UK
tel: 01845 524880
email: info@madeira.co.uk
www.madeira.co.uk
For Madeira stranded cotton (floss) and other embroidery supplies

Market Square (Warminster) Ltd
Wing Farm, Longbridge Deverill,, Warminster, Wiltshire BA12 7DD, UK
tel: 01985 841041
fax: 01985 541042
For work boxes and trinket boxes

MCG Textiles
13845 Magnolia Avenue, Chino, CA 91710 USA
tel: 909 591-6351
www.mcgtextiles.com
For cross stitch fabrics and pre-finished items

Sudberry House
12 Colton Road, East Lyme, CT 06333 USA
tel: 860 739 6951
email: sales@sudberry.com
www.sudberry.com
For quality wooden products for displaying needlework
Nantucket basket code 30015; lid code 30011

The WARM Company
954 East Union Street, Seattle WA 98122, USA
tel: 1 800 234 WARM
www.warmcompany.com
UK Distributor: W. Williams & Sons Ltd
tel: 017 263 7311
For polyester filling, cotton wadding (batting) and Steam-a-Seam fusible web

Zweigart/Joan Toggit Ltd
262 Old Brunswick Road, Suite E, Piscataway, NJ 08854-3756 USA
tel: 732 562 8888
email: info@zweigart.com
www.zweigart.com
For a large selection of cross stitch fabrics and pre-finished table linens

About the Author

Joan Elliott has been creating needlework designs for over 30 years, enchanting stitching enthusiasts the world over with her unique humour and charm. Design Works Crafts Inc. in the United States (see Suppliers) produce kits of many of her designs and she remains their leading artist.

Her debut book for David & Charles, *A Cross Stitcher's Oriental Odyssey* was followed by the equally successful *Cross Stitch Teddies* and her third book *Cross Stitch Sentiments and Sayings*, which allowed her to combine her creativity as an artist with her love of language to create projects that amuse, motivate and inspire all stitchers.

Native American Cross Stitch is her latest evocative collection of stunning designs, inspired by the distinctive and striking imagery of the Native American culture of her homeland.

Joan divides her time between New York City and Vermont and feels blessed that she and her husband have the opportunity to enjoy and share the many joys and experiences that both city and country life have to offer.

Acknowledgments

In recent years, with the work necessary to complete my books, I have come to know and enjoy wonderful relationships with the fourteen incredibly talented stitchers that worked the embroideries presented in this book. Each of my designs literally blossoms to life in their gifted hands. It takes my breath away when the packages arrive in the post and for the first time I see the completed embroideries in front of me. With love and gratitude to Rindy Richards, Bev Ritter, Judy Trochimiak, Lisa Rabon, Meem Breyer, Linda Steffen, Helen McClain, Lynda Moss, Mary Ann Stephens, Regina Kimbrell, Judy Suleski, Lois Schultz, Lori West, and Charlie Rosenberger. I thank you all.

Once again I want to extend my deepest appreciation to everyone at David & Charles whose efforts have made this book possible: To Pru Rogers for her beautiful book design and to Johnny Bouchier for his fine photography. I am especially grateful to Ame Verso for her incredible ability to keep track of everything involved in putting this all together. My thanks to Cheryl Brown who, knowing my fascination with Native American culture, had the vision to propose this book. Finally, a most special thanks to my editor, Lin Clements, whose friendship and support have carried me through once again. You are simply the best.

Index